OPTIONS TRADING FOR BEGINNERS:

Crash Course on Stock Market. How to Investing, Discover Advanced Strategies, Psychology. Tricks and Tips for Make a Living and Create a Passive Income from Home.

Introduction 1

Chapter 1: History of Options 7

Chapter 2: The Types of Options 13

Chapter 3: Options Trading vs. Day Trading 23

Chapter 4: Managing Options Positions 33

Chapter 5: Binary Options 56

Chapter 6: Trading Varying Time Frames 67

Chapter 7: Buying and Selling Puts 77

Chapter 8: How to Use the Collar Strategy 96

Chapter 9: Market Environment 111

Chapter 10: Rules for Successful Trading 122

Chapter 11: Tips for Trading Options 129

Conclusion 134

Introduction

Why trade options instead of the stock itself? As we'll learn later in this book, options can be used in a variety of ways to take advantage and profit from the inherent rise and fall of the markets. Options offer an array of solid trading strategies utilizing put and call options in abundant trade scenarios.

I'll mention one strategy in this chapter to show you how options can be used with your current stock trading, but we'll go into greater details in the strategy chapter. Options can be used to ensure your current holdings of stocks from a decline or increase, depending on if you are long or short. To explain the concept, you probably have insurance on your car or house against damage and loss of those assets. Options give the same type of safety net for stocks and investments.

Options offer protection against a market price decline of the underlying stock or an increase in the market price of the underlying stock, depending on if you are holding it long (speculating an increase) or short (speculating a decrease).

Options can facilitate a lower-priced stock purchase by exercising an in-the-money call option or sell a stock at a higher price by exercising an in-the-money put option. They can also provide an opportunity to create added income against a short or long stock position you are already holding. Here are some more reasons to start trading options, whether you have a stock portfolio or not:

Options Allow You to Trade
All Markets

No matter what the direction of the market is trending - up, down or sideways - there's always a strategy to use for option profits. Options can be traded in any sector offering option contracts.

Options Have Never Been Easier to Trade

In the past, people had to rely on newspapers and brokers to search for, find, and track their options trades, a system not always friendly to optimal profits. Today you can place and track your trades online and sell in practically an instant for maximum profits. There are websites to keep you informed without having to call your broker for the latest effecting news. Websites like www.cboe.com or www.finance.yahoo.com, list not only the stock's current price but also the option's current price and any news affecting the underlying stock, all in a matter of minutes.

Options Let You Start with Surprisingly Little Money

This is one of the best benefits of trading options versus stocks. You don't have to so much money to start. You can open a brokerage account with a minimal amount of money. Minimum required amounts to open an account vary from broker to broker, most brokers only require $1,000, and some no-frills brokers need less than $1,000, few require more than $2,500 so do your shopping! You can trade options in a retirement account with no minimum balance requirements with some brokers.

Options Provide Leverage, Safely

U.S. stocks are more expensive than ever before, and the large dollar investment required to participate in buying stocks really puts you and your money at the mercy of the market's constant churning, wreaking havoc on your portfolio and your emotions! Investors pay the price per share of the stock, whether it's $5, $100 or $1,000 per share. One hundred shares of a $5 stock would be $500, but a stock costing $100 per share is $10,000 and a $1,000 per share stock is $100,000. Whereas, options for the same stocks require 100 times less money for the right to control those shares. When the underlying stock prices rise or fall, the option prices rise and fall in relation to the stock price. This reaction can produce double or triple the money in profits. Below is an example of two stocks on each end of the expense spectrum and their correlating option prices for a current month expiration.

Amazon Stock:

Current stock price - $2,011 per share / 100 shares = *$201,100*

Amazon Option:

Current month expiration for an ITM option - giving the investor the option to buy the stock at a strike price of $2,000 and controls 100 shares.

Option price ITM- $27.75 x 100 = *$2,775.00* for the same 100 shares

Not all options are expensive as Amazon's, Cigna for example trades at $179.25 per share and its options trade at an ITM of $3.41 or an OTM of .59 = $341 and $59 per a 100-share contract controlling 100 shares.

The price quotes are for a 100-share control so you must multiply each price by 100 to calculate the dollar amount needed to buy one contract of 100 shares, if you wanted a 300-share control you would multiply the price quoted by 300 and so forth

Options Can Easily Double or Triple Your Money

You are using call options to profit from rising stocks and puts to profit from falling stocks. The best part is you can do it with far less money and double or triple your original investment without risking any more money than originally invested at the beginning. Options offer relief from high volatility in the markets, and the uncertainty of traditional stock investing methods.

Before we delve into option money making strategies, let's first go over the basics by learning option trading terms you'll need to know and how options actually work so that you can trade them smartly.

By knowing how options work and the terminology that's used, you will be better equipped to trade options profitably. Traders want to lose as little money as necessary and possible, and the less money you lose in this game, the more chances your portfolio will grow, and you will learn how to play it right. Losing a lot of money trading options, in the beginning, is more likely to compel you to quit before you learn how to play it correctly. Pay particular attention to the risk management chapter, and you will be rewarded with a deeply less concerning learning curve.

Chapter 1:
History of Options

Options trading and investing are growing at a record pace as interest among ordinary investors searches for speedy and safe ways to grow their portfolios. Options may be a new interest of yours, but the concept behind options has been around for thousands of years. Many have referenced an account found in Aristotle's "Politics" book published in 332 B.C., that's before Christ by the way! I'll tell you the story later, first let's fully fix in your mind what an option is, this way you will fully understand the value, leverage, and profit potential options offer.

Most people understand owning, buying, and selling stocks, so let's start there. You can buy or sell those shares, and you can collect dividends based on the number of shares you own. You control those shares or assets.

An option is the opportunity to buy the company's stock at a specified price and time, but not the obligation. In other words, you can if you want to and don't if you don't want to. You don't actually own any shares in the company, but you could.

Aristotle tells of a man named Thales of Miletus, an astronomer, philosopher and mathematician who studied the stars for weather patterns to determine that the ancient Greek olive harvest the following year would be a great one. Recognizing olive presses would be in high demand the following year, he sought to earn a huge profit by owning all or most of the presses but lacked the funds needed to secure numerous presses. Instead, he came up with the brilliant idea to pay a smaller amount of money as a deposit to secure the use of all the presses.

The harvest of olives that year, as predicted, went as well as he expected and those presses were in hot demand. He sold his right to the use of the presses to all the people who needed them, of course, turning a small amount of money into a large profit (leverage).

Thales controlled the olive presses (the underlying asset the option's based on), and he could use the presses himself, or he could sell his right of use to anyone needing a press and willing to pay more for that right, giving him a tidy profit. His actions defined how options worked down thru history and started the long history of options trading. Let's consider another example of options trading with the Tulip Mania that occurred in 1636.

The Ridiculously Priced Tulips Europeans Paid in 1636

Tulips imported from Holland and Turkey were so delightful that they became a symbol of affluence and soared in priced due to their demand. To grow a tulip, you must have a tulip bulb, and tulip growers experienced a need for a consistent and reliable flow of bulbs from their suppliers in Holland. Holland dealers, who were the biggest supplier of the quirky flower, started offering tulip bulb options to tulip producers, so they could secure the bulbs they desired and at the same time have a definite price, assuring the producers a way to fix their profits. This turned into a speculative play by all levels of society seeking investment returns. It's rumored many bought options with all they had, including selling or mortgaging their homes. But as all always happens, tulip prices had expanded so high that there was no longer any buyers at that exorbitant price and it quickly turned into a selling frenzy as option holders were wiped out during the mania, left holding expired or worthless option contracts. Notably, the Dutch economy collapsed as people lost homes and wealth. This is where options trading gained their infamous reputation for being a speculative and dangerous trading instrument.

London Declares Option Trading Illegal from 1733 to 1860

With the tulip mania of Europe still fresh in their minds, investors feared trading options. Still, a few financiers and speculative investors still traded and organized the options trading in London with the lesson learned from the tulip mania of 1636-1637. However, trading volume was low, and growing opposition eventually led to declaring option trading illegal in 1733. It remained illegal for over 100 years until 1860. Ignorance and fear can be a powerful driver!

1872, an American Rebirth of the Option and the Market Crash of 1884

In 1872 a well-known financier from New York was the first to venture into options trading in the U.S. by creating puts and calls to be traded on the NYSE. Russell Sage went from a political career to a financier in 1874 after buying a seat on the NYSE and offering options over the counter to investors willing to buy. Unfortunately, they were not standardized and could not be easily liquidated. Maybe this is the reason he died in 1906 with a $70 million fortune. Notably, too, he stopped trading options after he lost a fortune on them in the 1884 market crash. Nevertheless, the over-the-counter market for them continued to trade without him, albeit unregulated until the SEC was established after the great depression.

Efficiency thru Organization in 1973 with CBOE

Another hundred years of options trading went unchecked and perhaps unregulated until 1973 when the CBOE (Chicago Board of Exchange) stepped in along with the OCC (Options Clearing House) to define the way options are traded today. Some feel the most important role of the CBOE is the standardization of publicly traded options on a public exchange and how they are traded. Now all options have the same terms across the board and allow the public the ability to trade options alongside bigger investors. The OCC supplies a performance guarantee that gives the market liquidity under a market maker system. In 1977 put options were introduced by the CBOE and more options exchanges along the way which has led to better option pricing models and computation. The options market continues to evolve, but now with better regulation, options are standardized across the board, making options easier to trade and calculate profit potential along with risk.

Chapter 2:
The Types of Options

There are also two conventions that will be used when it comes to the options that you are using. If you are planning on just trading options in America, which is the only type of expiration that you will have to deal with. Some people like to work with international options as well, so it is a good idea to learn how both of these methods work:

- The European style expiry: the call options and the put options are denoted with the CE and PE. With this kind of expiry, your options are only exercised at the time specified for the expiry.
- The American style expiry: the call options and the put options are denoted with CA and PA in this method. For this kind of expiry, the options are going to be exercised at any time between when the option was purchased and when the expiry occurs.

The method that you are going to use will depend on what is considered the norm in the country where you are trading and where the stocks come from. For example, if you are trading options on the India NSE, you will want to follow the European style of expiry for results.

Short-term/long-term: All of the options that have been discussed up to this point have been what are known as short-term options. Long-term options tend to have termination periods that are years away which make them more useful for investors than traders. They are known as LEAPS or long-term equity anticipation securities and can be purchased just like any other type of option.

Option type by underlying asset

The most common form of underlying assets that the majority of options contracts are based on are the shares of a publicly listed company. But an underlying asset can take other varied forms, such as the following.

- *Index options:* These have a close similarity to stock options, except that the index, not the shares, is what the options are based on.
- *Forex/Currency options:* The contracts of this nature give the owner the authority to purchase or sell off a certain currency at an agreed rate of exchange.
- *Futures options:* The specified futures contract is the underlying security. A futures option allows the owner to enter into a specific futures contract.
- *Basket options:* The underlying asset can comprise a set of securities, such as currencies, stocks, commodities, and other financial securities.

- *Commodity options:* For this kind of contract, the underlying asset can be a commodity that is physical or based on futures contract.

Option type by expiration

Contracts can be categorized by their cycle of expiration. Some contracts have a fixed cycle while others are a bit more flexible. Below are some of the contract types.

- *Regular options:* These are based on standard expiration cycles that contracts are listed under.
- *Weekly options:* They are similar to regular options but have a shorter period of expiration.
- *Quarterly options:* They are listed on exchanges with expirations for the nearest four quarters plus the following year's final quarter.
- *Long-term expiration anticipation securities (LEAPS):* These expire in January, but they can be purchased with the expiration dates for the next three years.

ITM, OTM, and ATM Options

In the money (ITM), out of the money (OTM), and at the money (ATM) are three of the acronyms that you will hear about quite a bit when you are working with options trading (Thapar, 2018). ITM options are any that have an intrinsic value. If you exercise these options at that point, they are going to make you some money. Any call option that has a strike price less than the market price of the underlying stock it is considered an ITM option. On the other hand, any put option that has its strike price greater than the market price of the underlying stock will be considered an ITM option. The intrinsic value of any ITM option is going to be the positive difference between its strike price and the stock's market price.

To make it simple, when the price of the stock rises and crosses a particular strike price of its call option, then this option is going to become an ITM. Then when the price of the stock falls below the strike price of its put option, this option is going to become an ITM as well.

The OTM options are the opposite of the ITM options that we just discussed. These options are not going to have an intrinsic value. When they expire, all of the OTM options are going to be worthless. Any of the call options that contain a strike price that ends up higher than the market price of the stock and any put option that has a strike price that is lower than the stock's market price will be considered an OTM.

ATM options are going to be a bit different than the other two. These are going to be options where the strike price is the same as the market price of the stock. These ATM options can turn either into an ITM option or into an OTM option based on how the market prices end up changing over time.

Terms You Should Know

There are several elements or things that you are able to do when it comes to working with options, and it is likely that you will see a ton of terms as you get into the market. It is important to know what these terms all mean before you get into the market, or you will end up missing out on some important things that can help you make decisions. Some of the best terms that you should know when you are ready to join the options trading market include:

- The strike price (SP): every contract for options will have a strike price associated with it. This is the fixed reference price against which settlement takes place at the time the option is exercised or when the option expires. Of any of the given index or stock that is traded, there are going to be various options contracts that correspond with various strike prices. These prices are determined ahead of time by the stock exchange where the stock is traded.
- The lot size: the lot size specifies the fixed number of units of the security that your options contract is

17

covering. The regulatory body of the stock determines this lot size, and it is possible that the lot size can change based on the stock you are using.

- Premium: this is just the amount of money that the buyer of the option is going to pay per share when they are purchasing the option. So, the total cost of these contracts will be the premium multiplied by the lot size that you choose.

- Expiry date: every option that you work with is going to have an expiry date. This will vary depending on the contract, and it is possible that the expiry date could happen weekly, monthly, or even quarterly. You will know what the expiry date is when you purchase the options contract.

Understanding how each of these works can make a big difference in the experience that you have when it comes to working with options trading. Now that we know a bit of the basics, let's get into some of the other things that you need to work with in order to make money with options trading.

The broker

The success or failure of an options trader depends in large measure on the broker they are associated with. You have to select a broker that caters to your specific needs. For instance, if you're a beginner, you have to look for a broker that offers extensive educational resources and assists beginners through their early stage. Options brokers offer trades in common options and other tradable securities, such as stocks, mutual funds, exchange-traded funds, and bonds. An ideal options broker for a beginner-level trader must offer a low minimum and user-friendly platform. This will allow the beginner to adjust accordingly into the right trader's mindset without necessarily making costly mistakes.

A great options broker must have advanced research tools. The trader can select from a wide range of assets, and they should be able to do research so that they can make informed decisions. If you make your decisions based on misinformation and ignorance, it is obviously going to cost you. A great broker must also have superior trading tools. This is important as it helps to execute trades with much ease. Low commissions are important too as they increase the earnings of the trader.

The market maker

The work of market makers is to keep the financial markets efficient by ensuring a certain level of liquidity. They have contracts with various exchanges and they carry out large volumes of transactions. Market makers ensure that the market operates smoothly. They enable traders to buy and sell options even in the absence of public orders to match the required trade.

Market makers maintain an extensive portfolio of different options contracts. They are responsible for the depth and liquidity in the options exchanges. Without market makers, the options trading market would stagnate and traders would have a hard time. Considering the critical role that they play, market makers enjoy various privileges in the industry. The intention of each market maker is to make a two-sided market in the options of various securities. Thus, the market maker can buy from traders or sell to traders at any time. Market makers earn a profit from the price difference and considering the volatile nature of prices in the trading markets, the earning potential is pretty large. Large corporations seem to be slowly displacing the individuals who previously acted as market makers, as these corporations utilize expensive technology that automates the trading.

The Options Clearing Corporation

This organization is registered as a Derivatives Clearing Organization, and it's regulated by the Commodities Futures Trading Commission. The Options Clearing Corporation provides equity derivatives clearing and central counterparty clearing services. This organization is both the issuer and guarantor for options and futures contracts. It is the biggest financial derivatives clearing organization on the planet. The goal of this organization is to ensure that equity derivative exchanges are stable. The Options Clearing Corporation sees to it that all the requirements of the contracts it clears are met. This organization has held custody to an estimated $100 billion of collateral belonging to clearing members, and billions are transacted every day. The Options Clearing Corporation plays an indispensable function in the financial market, and it draws the largest percentage of its income from charging members. The organization also provides risk-control services. Its clients include professional traders, brokers, dealers, futures merchants, and other securities firms. By guaranteeing that transactions will take place as pledged, it promotes efficiency and orderliness in the derivatives market.
Options Industry Council

The Options Industry Council was first initiated in 1992 by the US options exchanges and the Options Clearing Corporation. Its main function is to educate investors and other parties in the financial sector about the advantages and shortcomings of equity options traded in an exchange. This cooperative is the industry's largest educational resource concerning equity options. Some of the large corporations that sponsor the Options Industry Council include the Boston Options Exchange, BATS Options, C2 Options Exchange Inc., the International Securities Exchange, the Chicago Board Options Exchange, Nasdaq Options Market, NASDAQ OMX PHLX, NYSE Arca, NYSE Ames, and the Options Clearing Corporation. The educational resources of the Options Industry Council may be accessed through online classes, podcasts, brochures, and DVDs.

Options are complex products. It's why the Options Industry Council (OIC) conducts hundreds of seminars throughout the year. Additionally, the OIC maintains a website that articulates everything about their educational resources. Most of their content is generated by experienced options industry professionals and then reviewed by compliance and legal entities to ensure that the message comes out as intended. Some of the materials provided at the OIC's website include options basics, trading strategies, advanced concepts, calculators, trading tools, trading data, newsroom, options store, and market quotes.

Chapter 3: Options Trading vs. Day Trading

Regardless of whether you are a broker or an investor, your goal is to profit. Your auxiliary goal is to do as such with the base worthy degree of risk.

One of the real troubles for new options brokers emerges originates from them not so much seeing how to utilize options to achieve their monetary objectives, since options exchange uniquely in contrast to stocks.

Everybody realizes that purchasing something now and selling it later at a more expensive rate is the way to benefits. In any case, that is not adequate for options dealers since alternative costs don't generally carry on true to form, and this hole in learning could make brokers leave cash on the table or bring about startling misfortunes.

Mathematical Tools by the Greeks

For instance, experienced stock brokers don't generally purchase stock. Now and again they realize undercut, wanting to benefit when the stock value decreases. Such a large number of fledgling choice brokers don't think about the idea of selling options (supported to restrict risk), as opposed to getting them. Options are uncommon investment instruments and there is undeniably more a merchant can do than basically purchase and sell singular options. Options have qualities that are not accessible somewhere else in the investment universe. For instance, there is a lot of scientific devices ("the Greeks") that merchants use to quantify risk. On the off chance that you don't get a handle on exactly how significant that is, consider this:

On the off chance that you can gauge risk (for example greatest addition or misfortune) for a given position, at that point you can likewise limit it. Interpretation: Traders can keep away from awful shocks by realizing how a lot of cash can be lost when the direst outcome imaginable happens.

Essentially, merchants must know the potential reward for any situation so as to decide if looking for that potential reward merits the risk required.

For instance, a couple of components that options dealers use to measure risk/compensate potential:

Holding a situation for a particular timeframe. In contrast to stock, all options lose an incentive over the long haul. The Greek letter "Theta" is utilized to depict how the entry of one day influences the estimation of a choice.

Delta estimates how a value change, either higher or lower, for basic stock or list influences the cost of an alternative.

Proceeded with value change. As a stock keeps on moving one way, the rate at which benefits or misfortunes aggregate changes. That is another method for saying that the alternative Delta is not consistent, however changes. The Greek, Gamma depicts the rate at which Delta changes. This is altogether different for stock (regardless of the stock value, the estimation of one portion of stock consistently changes by $5 when the stock value changes by $5) and the idea is something with which another options broker must be agreeable.

A changing unpredictability conditions. When trading stock, a progressively unstable market converts into bigger day by day value changes for stocks. In the options world, changing instability assumes a huge job in the evaluating of the options. Vega estimates how much the cost of a choice changes when evaluated unpredictability changes.

Supporting with Spreads

Options are frequently utilized in mix with different options (for example get one and sell another). That may sound befuddling, yet the general thought is basic: When you have a desire for the hidden resource conduct, for example,

Bullish

Bearish

Nonpartisan (expecting a range-bound market)

Ending up substantially more, or significantly less, unstable

You can build places that acquire cash when your desires work out. The quantity of potential blends is huge, and you can discover data on an assortment of choice methodologies that utilization spreads. Spreads have restricted risk and constrained prizes. In any case, in exchange for tolerating restricted benefits, spread trading accompanies its very own prizes, for example, an upgraded likelihood of winning cash. The fairly preservationist investor has a major favorable position when ready to claim places that accompany a good potential benefit - and a high likelihood of winning that benefit. Stock dealers have nothing like alternative spreads.

Options trading is not stock trading. For the informed alternative merchant, that is something to be thankful for on the grounds that choice methodologies can be intended to benefit from a wide assortment of securities exchange results. Also, that can be practiced with restricted risk.

When assessing how to invest in the market, you have options — both actually and allegorically.

You can purchase stocks, which speak to portions of proprietorship in individual organizations, or options, which let you wager on which course you think a stock cost is going. While there are significant contrasts among stocks and options — and the sort of investors who incline toward each — these benefits can supplement each other in your portfolio.

While finding intriguing investments inside the stock or options markets might offer, don't overlook minimal effort record assets and exchange-traded reserves, which pack various resources into one investment. Specialists for the most part prescribe that investors utilize these resources for structure the premise of a long haul portfolio — and they additionally fill in as a decent section point for novice investors.

In case you are determined to plunging into the market by means of stocks or options, which is okay. The rules underneath can enable you to settle on the correct decision.

Likely Disadvantages: Fees, Risk and Taxes

The risk related with stocks are direct: The cost could plunge to zero and you'd lose your whole investment. Since the presentation of individual stocks can be unpredictable every day, specialists by and large suggest investing in stocks with cash you won't requirement for in any event five years. To further diminish risk, don't heap all your cash into a solitary stock.

How dynamic a dealer you are will influence execution — and the amount you will pay in commission expenses and capital additions charge on benefits? Commission expenses for stock trading differ, so search around before opening a record. Your capital additions duty rate relies upon whether you understand a benefit on the closeout of the stock, to what extent you have held it — rates are higher for stock held not exactly a year — and your pay.

Options: Best for dynamic brokers who need adaptability

Searching for an increasingly strategic way to deal with investing, one with a littler investment prerequisite and adaptability in regards to timing or drawback risks? Options might be suited to your tastes.

With options, the related timeframe for investment is intrinsically shorter, making them all the more speaking to dealers who purchase and sell consistently. All options contracts have termination dates, which can go from days to years.

While numerous individuals like the adaptability managed by options — to be specific, time to perceive how an exchange plays out and the capacity to secure a cost without a commitment to purchase — they do add multifaceted nature to the investing procedure. Instead of settling on one choice, for example, wagering that a stock's cost will go up, you should make three:

What course the stock is going

How high or low it will move from its present cost

The time allotment where that will occur

That is options trading at its least complex; there are progressively confused methodologies for cutting edge brokers. There ought to be a decent hunger for investors to utilize options as a supporting device.

Options trading expects you to become familiar with another jargon of terms like puts, calls and strike costs, which may persuade these benefits are riskier than stocks. That idea is exaggerated, particularly in light of the fact that investors can allow a choice to terminate and cause no further budgetary commitment other than the premium paid and related trading costs. Likewise, long haul investors can utilize options as a kind of protection, he includes.

There ought to be a decent craving for investors to utilize options as a supporting instrument since it is a path for learners to get comfortable with options trading. Purchasing a put choice will help moderate potential misfortunes if the estimation of a stock you claim goes down. The value you pay for the choice, what's known as the premium, is similar to a protection premium, he says.

Likely Disadvantages: Additional Risk, Effort and Cost

Options trading requires a greater number of hands-on methodology than investing in stocks. You may wish to practice the choice before termination, and that implies you will need to watch out for the related stock's cost. You can set cautions through your online agent.

Likewise, a few options methodologies are riskier than others, so ensure you comprehend the exchange advance. Try not to decide on day by day or week by week options, which will in general be held for progressively prepared merchants. The more you exchange, the higher your expenses.

Another drawback of options trading is the related costs, which by and large are a lot higher than for stocks. Options dealers as a rule pay a level charge for every exchange, going from zero to $7 at the significant merchants, in addition to a for every agreement expense running from 20 pennies to 80 pennies. The more you exchange, the higher your expenses — and remember, you will pay charges to sell, as well. At last, similarly as with stocks, make sure to factor in capital additions charges. You will be on the snare to make good on regulatory expenses on benefits; these charges are higher for resources you have held not exactly a year.

Settling on your decision

Choosing whether stocks or options are better for you is completely an individual choice, in light of your investing style. Amateur investors and the individuals who lean toward effortlessness for the most part will adhere to stocks for their direct nature. The individuals who support a functioning investment approach and love to watch the market may discover options engaging.

In any case, don't accept you need to adhere to one resource. All things considered, options brokers intrinsically become stock investors in the event that they exercise call options. In the meantime, many stock merchants use put options as a supporting system. Whatever you choose, simply ensure you comprehend what you are doing first.

Chapter 4:
Managing Options Positions

How do you define your success? How do you manage your trading? Do you know anything about your options positions? Managing Option Positions are strategies that permit you to have follow-up action or to manage, to reduce or eliminate accrued losses, to help you protect any unrealized profits from your option positions. Different positions need to be examined to determine any follow-up action. This is warranted to know the performance of stocks since there is an initiated position. Moreover, it gives awareness about the revised forecast of traders about particular equity.

Rolling Positions

In options trading, there is the involvement of a rolling position. Rolling your trade will help you manage your losing or winning position. In rolling your trade, you need to close your existing position to open your new one simultaneously. You have the will to change your duration, strike, or both. As an options trader, you need to look at rolling as your defensive tactic and duration so you can achieve your success. You need to roll if you have the same assumption. When your assumption gets changed, you need to look further for your position, or you leave the risks that will easily spread and let the probabilities show up. It is subjective to know about rolling a trade. Thus, you need to look for many different aspects of trading to help you with your rolling position.

What can you do when you have profit probability lower than 33%? Or when you got previous trading's that repeatedly targeted profit? This is the best time that you'll need to roll your duration. Thus, there's no need to double your risk in doubling your contracts, and you need to roll for your small credit and duration. You will like rolling for your credit as it can add to your original potential profit and an extended breakeven price. In some situations, you do not need to look for risk trades that are so defined. You need to allow every possibility to show up and be comfortable with your trading.

Two Rolling Positions

- Rolling Up

This rolling position shows that you have swapped out an option that is a lower strike for contracts that have a much higher strike price. If you decided to play the call option, as well as your stock, then you made a dramatic and quick move from your side. It means rolling up is your way in raising your bullish stakes: selling the close with a prior call option on your profit, and buying a new strike call on a small capital. This is a great way to lock little gains form the initial trade. Thus, it makes you have a few fresh leverages in your profit from continuing higher moves.

Moreover, you can roll up when you had written your covered call as well as your stock make a higher move and cause you to have potential assignment risks. The strike higher call can be sold for open while the prior short option can be closed. Receiving credits is the best scenario that will be enough in offsetting your cost on both buy and close. Thus, it can give you some additional commissions and brokerage fees.

On top of that, these are only little examples as many other scenarios on rolling up can make sense. Instances like when selling your puts on the stock in betting your technical support, as well as your stock, had significantly risen higher. This could only mean that you can roll up in collecting a higher number of premiums.

- Rolling Down

This rolling position involves a closeout of the higher-strike option for exchanging your lower strike option. You have the will to select your roll down when you bought put options which significantly return as a gain in your side shortly after it was all initiated. When you sold your in-the-money options to close, then you have decided to exchange it for a cheaper put on the lower strike. This way, it can consistently move lower through your shares.

On top of that, you can roll down your short call position when your underlying stock is on a lower trend, or you need to roll down to your short put when your stock had dropped and hoped that you can avoid assignment.

Candlestick charts

Five Reasons Why You Should Learn to Read and Understand the Candlestick Chart

1. Through reading the candlestick chart, this will teach and give you tips to think about your probabilities.
2. This will help you to improve your many odds to win your trade extremely.
3. This will contribute to your learning about coming up with your analysis.
4. You will get to know those who are winning within the buyer's vs sellers.
5. You will use it as your blueprint for all your trading setups that you will trade.

Learn about the Part of the Candlestick: Open, High Price, Low Price, Close, and Range.

Before you get to understand the candlestick chart, first you need to understand the parts of the candlestick. The parts of the candlestick are the open, high, body, low, close including range. For instance, you will use the green one when your candle closes above or trading its open that is sometimes referred to as the Bullish candle. While if it is red colored candlesticks, it is due to your candle start closes or trading underneath its open or commonly referred to as the Bearish Candle.

- *Open*

This part shows your first price in the purchased of your candle's timeframe. Remember that when the following transactions are much higher than it's open. This only means that you should know that the candlesticks are color green. Once following trades after your open are below its open, this only means that the candlestick is turning red-colored.

- High Price

This will represent your highest traded price while the candle is on its timeframe or period. On top of that, it is shown through the upper shadow/wick. When you have noticed that there is no shadow or wick, it only means that either open price or close price has its highest price. This is important that you learn this part.

- Low Price

This will show your lower traded price while the candle is on its timeframe or period. Similar to the features of high price, you should notice the shadow or wick, yet you will see this on the candle's lower part. When you have seen that there is no shadow or wick, it only means that your close price has your lowest price. As a trader, you must be aware of your lower price.

- *Close*

This is considered as your last transaction or your last sold price in the candle's timeframe. It can completely determine your candle's color. If your traded last price had closed on your open, it only means that your candlestick must be green in color. On the other hand, when your last price is underneath your open, it only means your candlestick must be colored red. As a trader, you must know about it as you can determine whether your buyers or sellers won. Furthermore, the buyer is often called as bulls, and the seller is called bears.

- Shadows / Wick

If you are wondering those lines that display on the candle, it represents your high price as well as your lowest price. The difference is that the upper shadows or wick represent your high price, and the lower shadows or wick represents your low price. Remember that wicks depend on its length on the volatility.

- Range

The difference in the middle of your high price and lower price of your candlestick. If the range is bigger, it indicates a more volatile traded candlestick while it is on its timeframe. Also, it is on your buying pressure that is battling with your selling pressure. If the range is smaller, it indicates less volatility and can represent the consolidation. This is the formula that you can use in computing this: High Price − Low Price = Range

Candlestick patterns

The candlestick pattern in the technical analysis is referred to the prices' movement that is shown on the candlestick chart. Perhaps you will believe that this pattern predicts your specific market movement. Thus, the pattern's recognition is a program and subjective, that can be used in charting and needed to follow a predefined rule in matching the pattern. There are many different patterns that you can use to trade out with candlestick formations. It can help you have in as well as out in any trades with prudence and confidence.

You can combine reading trends, reading of learning how you can draw resistances and support, screen stocks, use the momentum indicators, utilize some indicators, risk management, and journaling. Then it will make way for you to be ready in coming up with your trading system. Lastly, you need to prepare for your trade after you have done proper testing with your strategy or set up. When you have already practiced your eyes on reading the candlesticks, the charting will be an easy task for you. You will never come into trading without keeping yourself ready to face any probabilities. Just keep in mind to be responsible for the decisions that you made in your trading and be diligent.

Example of Candlestick Patterns and Which One is The Best to Use

- Bullish Engulfing

Bullish Engulfing is a candlestick pattern that is seen in the chart's middle that comes in the blue box. This is a bullish reversal pattern that comes with a candle or two. This happens when the body of the candle completely engulfs the previous candle's body after its trend declined. This indicates that you have the high chance which buyers will be present, and the selling will continue. The following candles after this pattern indicate the presence of buyers.

- Evening Star

This candlestick pattern is considered a bearish reversal pattern. The evening star is a pattern that comes with a candle of three. Thus, it involves the prior uptrend. Its first candle shows bullish and strong. The middle one represents the trend's weakness; the last or third candle shows gaps down.

- *Harami*

Harami is a candlestick pattern containing two candles. The first one is bigger than the second one. The second candle, which is smaller stays in the first bigger candle's midriff. You must remember that the body is the only one who will need to put inside the prior candle due to the irrelevant wicks. The pattern of Harami is generally a changing sign on the trend, and it can be bearish or bullish.

- Three Line Strike

This reversal pattern is made of black candles of three around a downtrend. Every bar of it has a lower low post as well as its closes near its intra low bar. While its fourth bar had even opened lower yet need to revers on the outside bar's wide range which closes in series above the first candle's high. There is an opening print which marks the fourth bars low.

- Two Black Gapping

This is a bearish continuation pattern that shows a very notable top in the uptrend. Also, it has the gap down, which can yield black bars for two that post a lower low. Two Black Gapping can predict that there will be decline that will continue for some lower lows and it might trigger the broader scale of a downtrend. Moreover, it can predict the lower prices of about 68% of the accuracy rate.

- Three Black Crows

This is a bearish reversal pattern that near or starts at the high of the uptrend. It has black bars for three that post lower lows and close near at the intra low bars. Three Black Crows can predict the decline continues to be lower lows, and it might trigger the broader scale of the downtrend. Moreover, it can predict the lower prices of about 78% of the accuracy rate.

Reversal Patterns

The trading in a reversal pattern is mainly based on many patterns when there is a confirmation that shows a trend needs to be reversed. In identifying reversal patterns, you need to look at the big picture that is on the chart. On the other hand, you can also analyze 2-3 candlesticks.

List of the Big Picture on the Chart of a Reversal Pattern

- Double bottom or double top
- Triple bottom or triple top
- Bottom or top of shoulders and head
- Saucer bottom or saucer top

These are the candlestick patterns of bullish reversal:

- Hammer
- Bullish engulfing
- Bullish Harami
- Morning star

The list of few popular candlestick patterns of bearish reversal: Hanging man

- Bearish Harami
- Shooting star
- Evening star
- Bearish engulfing

Ordering Trade Steps in Reversal Pattern

These are the steps in a complete reversal pattern's chart, including triples or doubles, saucers, and head or shoulders.

- Step 1: Discover your potential pattern
- Step 2: Wait until your pair had move
- Step 3: Identify your neckline
- Step 4: Wait until your pair had broken its neckline
- Step 5: Wait for the confirmation of your pattern

Steps in Trading with Reversal Pattern

Once your technical pattern finally has done its confirmation, then you have to check your four points that left on your IDDA approach. Then you can now place your order.

- Up – New Trend
1. You need to place your order as a buy entry on the right above your neckline.

2. Then measure your distance from your pattern's lowest point to your neckline.
3. Remember that there will be an approximately moving in your pair that is equal to the distance of your previous afterward measurement.
4. Calculate your target price
5. You need to set your preferred trading limit on your calculated price.
6. The thing is not to be greedy!
7. Instead, wait until there is a move up on your pair against the price you have calculated.
8. There you go! You have made a little money trading on the bullish market.

- Down – New Trend

1. You need to place your order as sell entry on the right above your neckline.
2. Then measure your distance in the middle of your pattern's highest point and your neckline.
3. Remember that there will be an approximately moving in your pair that is equal to the distance of your previous afterward measurement.
4. Calculate your target price.
5. Set the stop in your calculated price.
6. Avoid being greedy!
7. You need to wait until there is a move down in against the price you have calculated.

8. There you go! You have made a few trading of your money on the bearish market.

Strategies in Trading with a Reversal Pattern

Sometimes, the price continues to move even if it had reached your target price. This means that you need to be a risk-taker and smart. Thus, you should not take nonessential risks and greediness. Here is the crucial thing you need to check in reality when you have invested in any asset:

Based on the approach of IDDA about strategy development, you must not rely on just a single method with your forex analysis. Instead, let alone a single method with your technical analysis. Sometimes, they will be biased even if you are on the best times on recognizing your forecast and identifying your reversal patterns. So, it is a must to use other analysis types and technical analysis tools in confirming your pattern. This only means that you need always to use the approach of IDDA in your every trading.

Trend continuation patterns

As an options trader, you must be familiar with many different trends. This can help you in your trading. Remember that there is more to do when traders are talking about trends. To go with the flow of other traders, you must look for your trend continuation patterns. While some traders fade, as they ignore those continuation patterns, then focus mainly on the reversal ones. There are not yet many different continuation patterns that provide technical analysis. There are still some that exist, and this is just enough for your option position.

You had a long journey in taking those technical analyses of continuation patterns, and this is the start of learning the different approaches such as the Western approach and Japanese approach. But here, I will focus on the Western approach.

These two approaches are different in many ways. Thus, there is the last one which is now becoming popular in the Western world. They still both complete their thing in each other. Many options traders, including you, must know these two.

You, as a trader, must have your favorite chart and this can be the candlesticks. Besides, the candlestick techniques of Japanese have the best continuation patterns for you. The Western approaches also offer different candlestick charts for all traders.

Do you know the generalities in continuation patterns? If not, then you must continue to read this. Here I will explain to you those generalities. You can just easily get this.

Just remember that every continuation pattern will show that the movement of the trends in similar directions. Or perhaps it might resume when the consolidation time ends. As the market moves its way or when the trend starts, take note that its way is not a straight line. Keep in mind that it takes a lot of time and effort due to several reasons such as no liquidity or there are only a few participants in the market. The technical analysis of the Western approaches is offering something to a trader like you.

This includes:
- Clear entries
- Measured move or take profit
- Stop loss

Moreover, I also want to share with you the trend continuation patterns in Bearish and Bullish Flags. Their flags always show continuity. Both bearish and bullish flags have to represent their continuation patterns. After your flag ends than it only means that your price breaks either lower or higher. In spite of your general brief, your flag must have three parts and not two.

- The pole
- Your flag
- Your move measured

Out of these three parts whether you want it, or you can't take it, yet your third one always matters. Perhaps, it is not seen as part of your flag, but if it is not interpreted correctly, this can lead to losses. Keep in mind that you should consider this first before anything else in your flag trading.

Perhaps, you wonder how you can trade your flag using the technical analysis of the continuation patterns. So, here I write down the information that can help you.

Many different books on technical analysis have been shown in the flag's pole. Thus, many options traders know it as the major feature.

Your pole shows a measured move. This only means that there is one way in trading your bullish flag though:
- You need to measure and look for its pole
- Place it on the break of your upper trend line
- Put the stop loss on the previous swing which is lower

It is not bad when you do your trading setup. This only means that you can have a reward of risk ratio that looks great. It is vital to make your trend healthy as it can help you break higher markets. An original setup of trading in continuation patterns which will surely help you in every trading you will do. Remember that it is essential to have your manager component in your money. Namely, each trade must contain:
- Take profit
- Stop loss
- The reward for risk ration which must be ideally more than 1:2

Demand and supply zones

Supply and demand zones can give your ideas about the different structure of the trading market. Through learning the demand and supply zones, you can be found that this is somehow similar to the resistance and support zones.

You will not be mistaken nor think twice when you have learned the concept about your demand and supply zones. There are specific rules that make these zones stand aside. Thus, it shines brighter than the resistance and support zones.

You can look for some examples of demanding and support zone on the internet where you can find that the options market of the German DAX. It comes with a red zone that is marked to be the supply zone. Sometimes it can deny as the active level of resistance or the place where some traders have sold bigger amounts. These zones are much broader than the resistance line. They similarly look like the resistance zones. Furthermore, most traders like you need to understand that the demand zone must have a broader support area.

You can find that these supply zones need more road level of support. Thus, it can be the concentrated level for buyers. You can also notice that when your price had approached its supply zone, it will immediately jump back above.

The last characteristic of the demand and supply zones is immediate price action. As we have mentioned, price action can be very fast within those levels. It means that when there are great opportunities, it will be quickly absorbed.

Maybe you will wonder how you, as a trader, can identify and look for your demand and supply zones. So, here I listed the following things that you must do to look for those four main types of demand and supply formations. As I pointed out at the top, you must follow these three steps to identify or look for your demand and supply zones.

- Look at your chart then try to look for successive large of successive candles.
- Establish your base
- Draw your zone

As already tackled about, it is difficult to draw your precise zone as it takes practice, effort, and most especially your time in spotting those areas. So, you need to follow those practices and rules completely until you become confident to reach new levels. Better to keep in mind that every successful options trader had followed these levels and had learned it successfully. Then as time pass by, you will surely become natural in quickly spotting these areas.

You can check out or find examples of demand and supply zones that available online or through trading books.

As an options trader, you must know that miracles do not exist in this kind of market. On top of that, demand and supply zones also have their disadvantages. In options trading, there is no such perfect tool or strategy. What makes to have difference is your overall attitude on your trading process. So, if you are just a beginner options trader in this market, you must know about these very crucial things that you need to pay special attention to:

1. Proper and effective trading education

This is a must for you if you are a beginner or even a pro. This trading education can help you to understand more about the concepts in trading.

2. The practice of trading (preferably on your Demo account)

3. Discipline on trading

4. Strictly follow your rules either it is good or bad days

5. Be open-minded

You must look for great possibilities and grab those opportunities that are given to you. This way you can choose the great trade you can have.

Biggest influences

As an options trader, you must know those biggest influences in your trading. This is an important thing for you as it might help you to have easy trading with other people. Perhaps you know that the most understood of the option influences is your underlying price. Most option traders are knowledgeable about the underlying option price along with their trades, and you must also be. The analysis in both fundamental and technical of your underlying option price are what you should understand.

As an options trader, whether you are a pro or a starter, you must be knowledgeable about the three factors that can influence your trading. The price influence will be at times, and it is easily understood. Some part of the influences is restrictedly forced to have unidirectional movement. There is a major reason why time can affect your option positions. Thus, it can significantly a result of its time or extrinsic premium's existence. Moreover, it depends on your risk profile on how you established your option strategy. Furthermore, the time passage can also influence your trade either positively or negatively.

Aside from that, the third option of price influence should also be your focus. It is crucial for you and can help you to have convenient trading. The implied volatility perhaps is the most overlooked and neglected component. The implied volatility can be taken with time, and this shows the time option premium's magnitude. Keep in mind that the implied volatility has its value as it can entirely inversely be connected to your underlying price. Thus, it can represent your aggregate view about the future underlying volatility. It is due that implied volatility can respond to your subjected view about future volatility. Consequently, the values can flow and ebb because of the future events that are expected to influence your prices, such as FDA decisions, earnings, and others.

As an options trader, you must practice being familiar with the options trading across the world. Moreover, you must spend time learning the influences of every option pricing. Besides, options markets will be hard for you when you had ignored its most significant influences.

Chapter 5: Binary Options

Binary options are similar to traditional options in many ways except that they ultimately boil down to a basic yes or no question. Instead of worrying about what exact price an underlying stock is going to have, a binary option only cares if it is going to be above one price at the time of its expiration. Traders then make their trades based on if they believe the answer is yes or no.

If you are currently considering trading in binary options, then it is also important to be aware that binary options trading outside of the US has a different structure. Also, when hedging or speculating, it is important to keep in mind that doing so is considered an exotic options trade, so the rules are different still. Regardless, the price of a binary options is always going to be somewhere between $0 and $100, it is also going to come with a bid price as well as an ask price, just like any other type of option.

They are also a great way for those who are interested in day-trading but do not have the serious capital required to get off the ground, to ply their trade. Traditional stock day trading limits do not apply to binary options, so you are allowed to start trading with just 1, $100 deposit. It is also important to keep in mind that binary options are a derivative created by its association with an underlying asset which means they do not give you ownership of that asset in any way. This means you cannot exercise them to generate dividends or enact voting rights as you would with standard options.

As an example, assume you are considering purchasing a binary option that states that the price of gold will be greater than $1,250 by $1:30 pm. If you believe the scenario is going to come true, then you would want to buy into the option. Otherwise, you would want to sell it. Further assume that the option is trading at a bid price of $42.50 and an ask price of $44.50, 30 minutes before it is set to expire. If you buy into the binary option at this point, you will pay $44.50. Otherwise, you would pay $42.50 to sell it.

If you buy in at $44.50 and then by 1:30 the price of gold is above $1,250, then your option would expire successfully and become worth $100. You would make a profit of $55.50 before fees are taken into account. If the price ends up lower than $1,250, then the option becomes worth $0, and you lose out on your $44.50.

Sooner or later, every option is either going to be worth $100 or be worth $0. The bid price and the ask price are set as the traders who are considering the trade determine the likelihood of success. The higher the bid and ask price are, the greater the overall perceived likelihood of the option coming true. If they are near 50, then the odds are average, and if they are very low then they are not skewed in favor of the average at all.

Where to trade binary options: Binary options are now traded on the Nadex exchange, the original exchange dedicated to legally selling binary options in the US. It offers browser-based trading via its own platform which offers real-time charts as well as market access to the latest binary options prices.

Binary options can also be traded via the Chicago Board Options Exchange (CBOE). It can be accessed with a brokerage account that is approved for options trading via their standard access routes. It is important to keep in mind, however, that not all brokers are equipped to offer options trading. As such, before you get started trading in options it is important that you make sure your broker offers all the trading possibilities that you may one day consider as changing horses mid-stream can be quite complicated.

Trading on the Nadex costs 90 cents when entering a trade and the same when exiting from one. The fee is capped at $9 per trade so purchasing a lot of 15 will still only cost $9. If you hold your trade until it expires then the fees will be taken out at that point. If the trade ends up being out of the money when it expires you will not be charged a fee. Trading via CBOE is handled through specific options brokers who charge a variety of different commission fees.

Choosing a binary market: You are free to trade in multiple classes of assets with binary options. Nadex allows for trading in all of the major indices including the Dow 30, Russell 2000, the Nasdaq 100 and the S&P 500. Global indices including those from Japan, Germany, and the UK are also available. Trades are also available for a variety of forex pairs including AUD/JPY, EUR/GBP, USD/CHF, GBP/JPY, USD/CAD, AUD/USD, EUR/JPY, USD/JPY, GBP/UDS AND EUR/USD.

Additionally, Nadex also offers trading in commodity binary options including soybeans, corn, copper, silver, gold, natural gas and crude oil. You are also provided with the option to trading based on specific news events. You can buy options based on whether the Federal Reserve is going to decrease or increase the rates of things like joblessness claims or whether or not the number of nonfarm payrolls is going to beat its estimates or not.

The BVOE offers a smaller variance of binary options to choose from that are not currently available anywhere else. There you can buy binary options based on their own interpretation of the current state of the S&P 500 and a volatility option index based on its own volatility index.

Risk and reward: Binary option risk is capped at the cost of the initial trade as the worst thing that will ever happen is that your option expires at 0. The risk is also capped, though it can still offer up significant returns depending on the amount of the initial investment. For example, if you purchase a binary option for $20, which ends up paying out, then you will still make $100 off of it ($80 profit) which means you have a 4:1 reward ratio which is more than you could find if you invested in the related stock directly.

This only works out in your favor to a point, however, as your gains will always top out at $100, no matter how much movement the underlying stock actually experienced. This downside can be mitigated to some extent simply by purchasing multiple options contracts up front.

Binary Option Strategies

Pinocchio strategy: This is the perfect strategy to put into play if you come across a candle bar with an extremely long wick and a very small body during the course of your technical analysis. This type of bar is known as a pin bar, but it was given its more descriptive name because the longer the wick grows, the more likely it is to be giving you false information.

If you come across this scenario and the wick is already quite long, then you can generally assume that the price of the underlying stock will have moved about as far as it can in the current direction and that it will likely be reversing quite soon. As such, when you see this bar then you will know that your best bet is to start trading against the majority as the trend is likely going to turn and benefit your new position. After the wick begins shrinking, you will then want to generate a prediction on a call, and if it begins to increase again, then you will want to change your prediction to a put.

Binary option reversal strategy: The effectiveness of this strategy is because the market naturally seeks balance which means that any price is bound to turn around eventually when confronted with extreme highs or lows. As such, when it comes to binary options, you can get a jump on the movement by predicting what is likely going to happen next.

For this strategy to work out effectively, you are going to need to predict the need for a put or a call based on the situation as it stands with help from information from external sources. You will find this to be a very useful strategy during periods of rapid asset movement because the speed at which it moves one way will be the same amount of speed with which it will eventually move back the other way. Because asset movement is bound to repeat itself eventually, once you understand its patterns you will be able to naturally tell when a given underlying asset is at its peak, making any relevant binary options a very clear-cut decision.

Martingale strategy: In scenarios where you are more or less unconfident in the current state of the market but still want to keep an eye on a given investment the martingale strategy can be quite useful. This strategy is also different than most other strategies as it involves heavily doubling down due to binary options' unique characteristics. As an example, if you start with a $20 binary option that does not pay out, then your next binary option should be worth $30 on the opposite side and so on and so forth until you make a profit. If your amounts get to the point where a $100 profit would not square you, then you would want to purchase multiple contracts at once.

This strategy is going to appeal to those who are naturally inclined to take risky investments that have a higher overall promise of return as well. With that being said, much of the risk can be minimized if you are familiar with the asset you are purchasing contracts on as you will already know the scope of the market and will not have to rely on the strategy to help you learn the ins and outs through unsuccessful contracts. This strategy is somewhat unique in that its odds of being successful are based almost entirely on your personal level of familiarity with the underlying asset.

Trade the news: Buying into binary options contracts for a variety of assets based on the news is an effective means of working with binary options that is more multifaceted than it may first appear. At its most basic, it involves purchasing contracts when good news is forthcoming and selling them when bad news is on the horizon. Unlike other types of analysis, it is much less of a science which goes in line with the more generalized nature of binary options in general. The most important thing you will need to learn to this type of analysis is how much of an effect a given piece of news is going to have on a specific underlying asset.

If you are fairly certain a specific piece of news is going to be released, and you are not sure how the market is going to react to it then the best way to ensure that you are going to end up making a profit is by setting up boundaries. To set up a bound binary option, all you need to do is pick 2 prices, one on either side of the current price of the underlying asset. As long as the price of the two is less than $50 combined you will still be making a reasonable profit, even after one of them expires at $0. The biggest risk with this strategy is that if the price does not move at all then you both binary options are likely to expire at $0, costing you both the entry fees in the process.

Trading the breakout, the period right after the news has been released is another useful way to take advantage of crucial news whose effect was unclear prior to it being released. While this is a strategy you will no doubt see with many types of investments, it is especially challenging to use when working with binary options as the window for success can be as small as just 30 seconds, while never being larger than a few minutes.

The most prominent swings in asset price are going to happen during this period, so you will need to be prepared for this fact and ready to quickly jump on binary options created by traders who are looking to modify their positions in hopes of minimizing their own risk. As long as you have done your homework, and have a clear idea of what the news is likely to be, then you will then be able to buy into extremely short 60-second binary options and take advantage of all of the confusion.

Finally, if you are comfortable with technical analysis, then you will likely be able to take advantage of candlestick formations to help you trade the news more effectively. When you come across a candlestick with a gap in it, then you can safely assume that the price of that particular asset will have moved quickly from one point to another that is either much higher or lower to create it. As this much movement, all at once, is relatively uncommon, coming across one should be enough to give you pause and cause you to look at the asset that caused the gap more closely.

Over time, you will find that identifying the gap early on will allow you to make a wide variety of different predictions based on what the market was up to at the time. These include:

- If the gap is created during a period of low trading volume, then it is likely that the gap price will be corrected very quickly. This type of gap is generally formed after a large trade goes through after most of the institutional traders have called it a day. This means that the change does not actually reflect the strengths of the underlying asset so that you can easily set up binary contracts that take advantage of the fact that things will soon be moving back towards normal.

- If the gap occurs during a stretch where overall trade volume is up, but the movement on the underlying asset in question has been neutral then this can be thought of as a strong indicator that a new breakout is occurring which means that the potential for profits is increased. If you move quickly, you can take advantage of this fact by buying into contracts that line up with the direction the breakout indicates.

- Finally, if the gap appears during a space of average trading volume when the asset in question is already moving in a given direction, then the gap can be thought of as a sign that the trend that it is being monitored is accelerating. This, in turn, means that the trend is likely to continue, at least in the short-term. You will only want to be comfortable assuming the trend is going to last into a longer time frame if ancillary indicators are very strong.

Chapter 6: Trading Varying Time Frames

Weekly Options Trading

Weekly options are listings which provide an opportunity for short-term trading as well as plenty of hedging possibilities. As the name states, they have an expiration time of exactly one week; in general, they are listed on Thursday and expire the following Friday. While they have been around for decades, in the past they have primarily been the domain of investors who work with cash indices. This level of exclusivity changed in 2011 when the Chicago Board of Options expanded the number of ways they could be traded, especially to make them more easily acceptable to traders like you. Since then, the number of stocks that can be traded weekly has grown from 28 to nearly 1,000. In addition to having a short time frame, weekly options differ from traditional options in that they are only available 3 weeks out of the month. They are also never listed in the monthly expiration style. In fact, the week that monthly options expire, they are technically the same as weekly options.

Advantages of weekly options: The biggest benefit of buying into weekly options is the fact you are free to purchase exactly what you need for the exact trade you are looking to make without having to worry about coming up with extra capital or dealing with more options than you currently need. This means if you are looking to start a swing trade, or even an intraday trade, weekly options will have you covered. For those looking to sell, weekly options provide the ability to do so more frequently, rather than having to wait a month between sales.

Weekly options trades are also useful in that they lead to reduced costs for trades that have longer spreads, such as diagonal spreads or calendar spreads as they can sell weekly options against them. They are also useful to higher volume trades as they are useful when it comes to hedging larger positions and portfolios against potential risky events. Also, when the market is range bound the weekly options, market can still be utilized through means such as the iron butterfly or iron condor.

Disadvantages: The biggest disadvantage when it comes to weekly options is the fact that you will not ever have very much time for a trade to turn around if you make the wrong choice in the first place. If you are selling options, then you will also need to know that their gamma will also be much more sensitive than it would be with more traditional options. This means that if you are planning to short options, then a relatively small move overall can still lead to an out of the money option entering into the money very quickly.

Weekly options are also known to require a good deal more micromanaging of risk. Without taking the time to size your trades and guarantee your profits properly, you will find that your available trade balance disappears quite quickly. Furthermore, the implied volatility of all of your trades is going to much higher than it would have been otherwise due to the time frame you are dealing with. Near term, options are always going to be more open to large price swings as well.

Buying weekly: Because you are always going to have much less time when it comes to turning a profit with a weekly option, your timing for when to move on a specific decision is going to need to be much more precise than it would otherwise have to be. If you choose poorly at either strike selection, time frame or price direction then you can easily find yourself paying for an option that is generally worthless. You will also need to take into account your level of acceptable risk as the option is going to be cheaper per unit, but you are going to need to purchase more in a week's time than you otherwise would.

Also, it is important to avoid making naked calls or puts when trading on a weekly basis as these typically work out to be lower probability trades as a whole. If you have a bias when it comes to the direction you want your trades to move in, then using a debit spread or structured trade is generally preferred.

Selling weekly: Selling reliably for the long-term can generate steady profits if done properly. It only works this way if you are defining your profits up front, which means it is important to always know what your options are worth to prevent you from selling yourself short. Selling trades weekly will make it easier to collect the full premium if they guess correctly while still leaving you exposed to unmitigated losses if you choose poorly which requires an extra margin.

The ideal types of underlying stock to use for these types of trades is going to be lower priced as they each ultimately consume a smaller amount of your total buying power. This also means it is easier to move forward on trades with lots of implied volatility as it is more likely to revert to the mean in the allotted time. As a rule, selling a put in the short-term is always better than selling a call as it tends to generate an overall higher return in the shorter period.

Spreads: Spreads are a great way of making a profit in the weekly market. The overall level of implied volatility is going to be much higher in the weekly market than in the monthly variation so the spread can help you when you find yourself dealing with an unexpected directional change quickly enough that you can actually do something about it. Selling an option against a long option will naturally decrease the role volatility plays in the transaction. The best point to use the debt spread will be near where the price currently is, providing you with a 1 to 1 risk and reward ratio.

Intraday Trades

While options are frequently left out of day trading strategies, this trend is slowly changing. Traders are slowly but surely realizing that they can apply many standard day trading techniques when it comes to selling and buying options successfully.

Intraday trading challenges: When attempting to day trade options, you are likely going to run into some unique challenges, that you should be able to best with the proper consideration.

1. Price movement will decrease value more significantly due to the time value naturally associated with options that are only near the money so close to their period of expiration. Remember, while their inherent value is likely to increase along with the underlying stock price, which will be dramatically countered by the time value loss.

2. The bid-ask spreads are typically going to be wider than they would otherwise be which is due to the reduced liquidity that you will typically find with the options market. This will frequently vary by as much as .5 of a point which can cut into profits if things move at an inopportune time.

Some types of options are naturally a better fit when it comes to day trading than others. Perhaps the most effective is the near month in the money option which is appropriate for those traders who are a fan of trading stocks with a high level of liquidity. The premium on this type of option is based more closely on its overall value as it is already in the money and getting close to its expiration date. If this occurs, the time value drain is decreased dramatically. This type of option is generally traded most effectively in periods of high volume which tends to result in a decrease in the gap between asking price and bidding price.

Protective put: The protective put is a type of option that is useful when you purchase put orders along with shares of the related underlying stock. This is a reliable strategy when the underlying stock is likely to experience a high degree of volatility. It is especially effective when used to purchase the same option throughout the day to continue to capitalize on short bursts of positive movement. It is also useful when it comes to providing insurance when purchasing shares of a risky underlying stock as you will always be limited in your potential losses to the price of the options you purchased.

Protective puts are also useful in a strategy known as bottom fishing. It is common for many underlying stocks to regularly break through existing support levels and continue moving down into an entirely new lower trading range. When this occurs, it is in your best interest to seek out the bottom point of the downturn so that you can catch it before it starts moving back up. This is easier said than done, however, as it is possible for a stock to give off false signs of having hit bottom and buying in at that point will only lead to serious losses. This is where the protective put comes in, however, and limits the possibility for risk substantially.

While there are models that can be used to calculate the likelihood of the bottom of a given trend, they too can be fooled by the exhausted behavior, which can indicate a false bottom. As such, when you feel that a given stock has bottomed out, then you can buy in with a protective put and then be protected regardless of the ultimate outcome.

Directional options trading: The most effective directional strategies when it comes to intraday options trading are those which have the overall highest degree of making it possible to make quickly moves time and again. These moves are typically going to occur at specific retracement levels or around breakouts.

- Trades that are based around the Fibonacci retracement on the charts for time frames less than 10 minutes. Fibonacci retracements can be used to determine reasonable reward/risk levels either by selling a credit spread to the level in question or through buying options that are already in the money that are likely to experience a bounce at these levels. It is generally going to be in your best interest to look for Fibonacci levels that are likely to overlap at multiple time frames as well as corresponding to the most recent trend experienced by the underlying stock. If you are so inclined, you can also utilize candlestick price patterns as a means of confirming a buy at specific Fibonacci levels.

- Alternately, you may find success with oversold or overbought indicators when it comes to range-bound or trendless stocks. You can then sell credit spreads or buy into options that are already in the money and near the current level of resistance and support with tight stops. It is important to keep in mind that a given stock might not move quickly enough to make these levels worthwhile, so it is important to do your research ahead of time to have a reasonable expectation about the future movement.
- Indicators that are used to signal lower than average volatility such as Bollinger bands are especially useful when it comes to place trades that you anticipate big moves from. Breakout indicators time, especially for the shorter charts, are also especially useful.

High volatility options intraday strategy: Trading volatility by selling options with high volatility, such as credit spreads that are currently out of the money will allow you to make a profit when anticipating a volatility drop. This is a commonly used professional strategy to employ when it comes to earning season or other scenarios where the underlying stock has developed a big price gap. The front month short-term options will then have an extra-large amount of volatility that makes it easier to generate a positive reward and risk ratio when selling. The most common way to take advantage of this fact is through utilizing an iron condor with strike prices of the earning move that is expected to be forthcoming.

Then, before the earnings numbers are announced, you then look up the premiums of at the money calls and get an early idea of what the major players are expecting when it comes to the earnings. This will allow you to determine where you are going to want to place your put credit spread at along with your call credit spread as well. If the stop gap ends up either too low or too high from the expected range, then you still get to keep the premiums. This strategy essentially allows you to trade the way a market maker would through the use of probabilities.

Chapter 7:
Buying and Selling Puts

Next, let's talk about buying and selling puts. Puts, of course, allow you to sell the stock that you have or the underlying commodity that you have underneath it all. There are different reasons why people may want to buy or sell puts, and here we'll go over what it is, how to do it, and the advantages of such.

What is Buying and Selling Puts?

Selling/buying puts essentially is giving someone the option to buy the stock at a certain amount of money.

If you sell a put option, you're selling the chance for someone to buy that stock at a price.

If you buy a put option, you're giving someone the option to buy that stock for that price and the person is obligated to sell it.

So, let's say that you're planning on getting a put option to buy that stock at a certain amount of money. You can put that option down, and from there, wait for it to fall, and from there you can exercise it. Maybe you want to buy shares from a really good railroad company. You essentially notice it's increasing the earnings on this, and you decide to potentially buy the stock when it's under 30. By buying a put option, it basically makes the seller obligated to sell you the stock when it falls below 30 dollars.

You want to exercise these in falling markets since you'll generate a profit when the market is falling, rather than rising.

Selling Puts in this Market

Here's the thing, when you want to sell puts, you should only do so if you're comfy with the owning stock that's under it at the price that's there because essentially, you're assuming the obligation to buy it if the person does decide to sell. From this, you should also only enter trades where the net price paid for the security is good. This is the most important part of selling puts profitably in the markets that you have. There are other reasons to sell it to the person. You also can own the security below the market price that is currently there, and you'll definitely want to be careful when you do choose to sell this.

An Example of Buying a Put

Let us now move onto buying these puts. One thing to note is that you're not going to see the commissions, taxes, margins, and other charges factored into any of these equations for a reason. That starts to get it a bit more complicated, and right now, we are just showing you the cut and dry of all of the ways you can buy a put option that can be considered. But, you should definitely consult with your tax advisor or broker before you go in.

So the simplest way to bet against stocks is to get put options. Put options essentially give you that right to sell it at a certain price by a time period. You essentially pay the premium, which will from there will sell you that stock at that price.

So let's say you've got company A, which is overvalued currently at $50 bucks a share, and you decide to bet on a decline at this point, getting a put contract that's at $35 a share, and it costs $2 per share, so the "breakeven" price is $33 a share. This is deduced from basic math, since you're taking the contract price of 35 minus the 2 making it $33 for this. Since each of these represents 100 different shares. That's $3500 in total of what you'll buy, and then of course it'll cost you upfront $200 for this (cause of the options contract and the shares) and from there, you enter the trade.

Now, let's say that the option contract is for August 2019, and from there, you fast-forward and watch the market. Below is a table of what can happen

Action of stock	What happens to you	Your return	Outlook
Soars all the way up to $60	The option expires, becomes worthless, and you lose the $200 premium, but you're basically losing nothing else	(100%)	Okay
Falls slightly to $38	Same thing happens, stock falls but you don't make a profit	(100%)	Okay
Drops all the way to $25	You make some cash! 800 dollars to be exact ($35-25) and then the $2 premium	(800%)	Nice!
Drops to $0 (basically going bankrupt)	The ideal situation, and you'll get $3300 from it (0 at expiration, so 3500-200 from the premium)	(1500%)	Ideal!

So the best time to use these is when you have a sinking ship in terms of stock. Otherwise, they aren't worth your time, and it's better to not have these stocks, and there is always a chance you could end up losing money. But, if the person sells the stock, and you turn around and cash in on it, you'll have more money, and you don't have to worry about the burden of a stock.

If you choose to buy it when it declines, you're essentially going to get money from this. You want to do it when it's declining and nothing more. It is very important that you don't choose to act on these types of options until it's that time.

That's it, that's all buying put options is, and you want to make sure that it falls to the level that you want it to be at.

The risks of it

Risks are still there in both cases. Options are risky due to the complex nature of this, but once you know how these works, it can reduce the risk a whole lot. Put options, in particular, can be quite risky, especially for the seller, since they may have to spend more money buying back the option that they once had.

One other aspect of this, especially for buyers is the break-even aspects of it. So, let's assume that you got a stock today for $46 and this was at $44, which is two points down what it is there, so you'll be profitable in the trade. But, here's the thing, you're going end up losing out on money due to the fee for the option. It would make the option worth $2 since you spent $4 on it, so that means you're losing out on it.

But there is also the fact that if the option does expire and you're in-the-money, you'll get the right stock immediately. You may not realize it, but these can be quite good, especially for plunging markets, especially if you know they will bounce back.

If you end up seeing it go high, you're going to end up paying for that premium to get the right to buy it, and that's money that can rack up to a couple of thousand dollars. Do make sure that you understand that when you do choose to figure out your own stock, and how you can easily rectify.

The Advantages of Buying Puts

Buying puts, which gives you an option to sell the stock at a given price, is good if you're looking to protect yourself. So let's say that you have this stock, or you've been eyeing a stock that will probably fall, and then rise over the next few months. There are those out there, and usually, it's due to lulls in the market at the time. So, you decide to buy the put that's there, which gives you the option to sell that stock when the market decides to resurface at a higher level.

For you, you're taking a gamble on this, because the market may not recover, but if you notice a stock that could potentially have the power to possibly fall, this may be a good one. That way, you can get the stock for cheaper. From there, you can sell the stock again, and you have the right to sell that stock at the price that you're looking for.

It essentially allows you to form that extra security in his, which is a nice little advantage for the person who wants to sell it. Long puts are good for this, especially if you want to sell these.

Put options let you sell this asset at the strike price that's there. With this, the seller is then obligated to purchase these shares from the holder. Now, how can this help? Let's say that you buy a stock at 20 bucks, and then you compare it to 20 dollars at the edge that's there. If the price is below 20 at any point, you can actually then exercise the options and reduce the losses. This can definitely help, especially if you're willing to buy an option, and from there, sell it in order to avoid lots of trouble.

Naked Puts

There are also naked puts, which is an advanced put options strategy, so I don't suggest trying this till you've worked with basic puts. The reason for that is because of their incredibly risky.

What does it mean to trade an option naked though? It doesn't mean that you're going to the stock exchange in the buff, but rather, you're selling the options without having a position in the underlying instrument. For example, if you're writing a naked put, you're selling a put without having the stock.

The covered call is probably the most basic stock trading strategy. This strategy provides an ideal entry point for those who are new to options trading and allows them to turn their existing investment activities into a gateway for trading options. The premise of the covered call is quite simple. The idea behind this strategy is to minimize your cost basis on your stock purchases.

Let's take a look at how this works.

Covered Call Strategy

The best way to think about a covered call is to look at it as a method to earn dividends on your stock holdings. While a stock may or may not pay you a dividend, with a covered call strategy you can earn income on the position and therefore lower your effective purchase price. Another way of looking at this is to view it as turning your stock purchase into a bond which pays you monthly or bi-monthly interest.

So how does it work? Well, the strategy has two legs to it.

1. A long stock
2. A short call

Execution

The long stock leg is simply your investment purchase in a stock. A lot of people who get into trading already hold shares as part of a retirement account or some other portfolio. If you already hold a position in some stock, then employing this strategy will work wonders for you.

The execution is pretty straightforward. You already hold long stock or establish a long stock position in some company that you think has good long-term prospects. I must emphasize that this leg is all about investment and it has nothing to do with speculation. Whatever research you do to purchase this stock should be done on the basis of sound investment principles. So you need to be aware of the earning ability of the company and its long term prospects. Do not purchase stock just to execute a covered call.

The short call simply provides short term income against your long term holding. So really, it's an appendage to the original position and gives you some cash in the short term while you're invested for the long-term capital gain. I know I'm repeating myself here but this is because a lot of beginners think a covered call is a speculative strategy.

The truth is that one leg is speculative while the other is based on investment principles. If you're not aware of the differences in mindset and goals between investment and speculation then I suggest you do your homework in this regard. Anyway, let's get back to our strategy.

The idea is to write an out of the money call which will be covered by the stock position. Remember how I said that writing calls is extremely risky business? Well, with this strategy the long position 'covers' your written call, hence the name covered call. When choosing a level to write a call, you need to pick one which you think will not be hit or in other words, a level which will not move into the money.

I'm saying this because your objective should be to preserve your long-term stock position. After all, if it is an investment, you want to hold on to it for as long as possible. It's true that even if your written call moves into the money and gets exercised, you're not going to suffer a major loss since you'll be selling your stock at a higher price anyway.

However, your biggest cost will be the opportunity cost of losing the long position. Assuming the stock has moved into a level which is far out of the money, this means it has significant bullish force behind it. In such cases, the capital gains you can experience by just holding onto the long position will dwarf whatever premium you earn by writing the stock. So do keep this in mind when writing the call.

Can you use this strategy for short term speculation? Well, you can but there's not much upside to it. If you're a regular directional speculator, this strategy will increase your short-term gains. However, in speculation, the objective is usually to reach a desired profit target and then exit. Given the usual speculative holding times of up to a week, a covered call doesn't really make sense.

This is because you want to write options which are expiring at least a month from your trade date. Why a month? Well, remember the time value portion of the option price? This will be at its highest when the expiration date is at least thirty days away. When the expiry date moves to within a month, the time value exponentially decreases. Thus, your premium earned will be far lower the shorter your holding times.

The position should last you a little over a month and to execute this you should write options for the near month (that is, those that expire in the month after the current one). So let's look at how the math works out via an example.

Example

For the remainder of this book, I'm going to use the options chain prices of Google. The options chain refers to the prices of the calls and puts for various strike prices. The table of prices is displayed vertically and is hence called a chain. Remember when looking at the premium prices to pay attention to the expiry dates.

In most trading platforms, you first need to choose your expiry date via a dropdown and then the calls are usually listed on the left of a table with their strike prices next to them and puts on the right. Alternatively, some platforms display calls on top and puts at the bottom. Lastly, remember that when you buy an instrument in the stock market (or any financial market), you'll need to pay the ask and when selling, you need to pay the bid. The bid and the ask will be listed as separate columns for each strike price.

Well that was a mouthful. So, back to GOOG's options chain. The current trading price of GOOG is $1229. Let's say you bought this position some time back at the price of $1200 which means you're sitting on an unrealized gain of $29. You've studied the charts and think that the long-term prospects of GOOG are good but you'd like to earn some income from this position. Think of it as earning rent on a property you've purchased.

You head over to your terminal and look at options expiring the following month. You'll see four choices of expiry dates for October (I'm writing this in September), the 4th, 11th, 18th, and 25th. We want to choose something that is at least thirty days away, so let's go for the 25th which is more than this amount of time away.

Next, you need to decide on an appropriate strike price. Remember, you want this price to be far enough away so that it doesn't move into the money. However, if you choose something that is too far away, the premium you earn will be less. So you need to balance the two. This is why I stressed earlier that the objective is to earn interest on this trade, not to make a huge profit. If you go in with the latter mindset, you're likely to pick something that's far too close to the current price. As a result, you'll lose your long position and find that your premium doesn't really make up for the opportunity cost.

So how should you think about picking an appropriate strike price? Well, use the principles of support and resistance to begin with. Is GOOG nearing a resistance? What is the closest strong resistance in its path that will ensure GOOG will not break through immediately? Next, analyze its historical performance. When I say historical, I mean the past few months, going back for up to a year.

How much on average has the stock risen in this time? Let's say GOOG has risen on average 3% whenever it has gone up. Remember to not include the months where GOOG has declined in this calculation. The point is to figure out how much it usually rises whenever it goes up.

Assuming things stay relatively the same, 3% of 1229 is 1266. So we can use this as a decent ceiling. If this price happens to fall beyond a resistance one, then even better. Next, you need to look at the fundamental factors, in terms of events. Are there any special announcements due over the next month? If GOOG is going to be announcing its quarterly earnings during this period, write a call that's more than double the monthly movement away.

GOOG is a tech company so is there some tech conference coming up where they're expected to make a major announcement? Have they been caught selling people's data to someone, like Facebook recently was caught doing? While some of this is unpredictable, your aim should be to understand whatever is available at this moment.

This is to account for any volatility that will occur following the announcement. Once you've done this, review the strike price in terms of s/r once again. The combination of s/r, fundamental factors and historical monthly rise should inform your strike price. In this case, let's say 1270 is a good level to write a call at. This is not a recommendation by the way, I'm simply using this level to highlight the example.

Heading over to the option chain of GOOG we see that the 1270 October 25th call can be written for $16. So you'll earn this amount when you write the option. So whatever happens now, you've added $16 to your overall profit from this position.

Let's say GOOG moves into the money despite your best efforts. Well, you keep the call premium no matter what. However, you have to let go of the long position. You bought the stock at $1200 and will have to sell it at $1270 since this is the strike price of the call. So, your long position nets you $70 as profit. Your short call yielded $16 as profit. All in all, you've cleared $86 per share as profit on your position. Remember, this is the worst-case scenario.

If GOOG declines below your purchase price, well, you're in this for the long haul and your investment horizon is for decades, not for a few weeks. So you should be able to stomach any unrealized losses. Meanwhile, you earn the premium. The best-case scenario is if GOOG rises to a level below 1270. This way you've earned an unrealized capital gain as well as the premium. Either way, what the long stock position does should not concern you beyond the fact that it crosses 1269.9 or not. Whatever else it does, you'll be fine. As you can see, the covered call is a fantastic way to make money on an existing purchase.

If you wish to take more risk, you can choose a strike price that's closer. Let's say you're feeling particularly daring and choose 1255 as your strike price. In this case you'll earn $21 per share when you write your call.

How much risk you wish to take is up to you. Remember that this is not a major gain strategy but is an interest producing one. In the case of the 1270 strike, you'll earn $16 per share on an initial investment of $1200. That's a monthly return of 1.3%. If you can keep this up throughout the year, you'll earn 16% before taxes and commissions. Let's see a real estate investment give you that!

Other Considerations

The biggest income generator in this strategy is the time value that's built into the option. Consider this: Let's say we stick with the 1270 strike but play around with the expiration date. What are the premiums we would earn for strike dates that are closer than the one on October 25th?

Well, the calls expiring on September 20th, which is less than a week away, will yield you a princely sum of $0.19. September 27th will yield you $1.40. Things get a little better in October. October 4th gives us $4.80. October 11th nets us $6.90 and finally, October 18th, which is about a week apart from our choice of October 25th, will yield us $9.91.

So a difference of a week results in a premium decrease from $16 to $9.91. That's a 38% price drop! Hopefully now you can see my point about the value of time decay. It decreases exponentially and thus you should take full advantage of it. If time decay decreases exponentially, surely it makes sense to pick an expiry date that is as far away as possible? Well, let's see how this plays out.

November 15th's 1270 calls are priced at $25.40. December 20th is at $38.30. January 17th will yield you $44.30, March 20th yields $67.20 and June 19th yields $89.80.

As fast as the premium decreases, so does it increase the further out your dates are? Given this information, surely you ought to be rushing writing the June 19th calls? Well, not so fast. There are some considerations to take into account. First, are you sure GOOG won't hit that strike price before that date? Second, what does your overall return profile look like?

If you write the June 19th call, your annualized return is only going to be around 11%. Remember, this is before commissions and taxes. If you write the November 15th call, your annualized return increases to 13% but is still well below the 16% you earn from writing October 25th's calls.

The reason the near month calls yield the highest is due to the fact that the Black Scholes model, which is used to price options, just has more information the closer the expiration date is. It can predict things better. Furthermore, you'll have greater liquidity the closer your expiration date is.

You're familiar with volatility, so let's now meet the other major stock market phenomenon. Liquidity simply refers to how much trading volume is present. In other words, is there an active market for a stock at a given price? Stocks that see low volume are illiquid. Liquidity is a major concern because the lesser the number of trader's present, the easier it is to get a worse price.

Think of it this way. If you're selling your car but there's just one dealer in town, you'll be forced to accept whatever price they offer you. If there are two dealers, you're less likely to get screwed. The greater the number of dealers, the better your chances of getting a fair price. Substitute dealers for traders and you'll see what happens in the stock market.

Options which are farther out tend to have less liquidity. Therefore, you're forced to take whatever price you receive and this can lead you to earn far less than what you might have gotten otherwise. This is why the October 25th calls are in a really sweet spot. They're just far away enough to still have time value, but close enough to have good trading volume in them and hence you're going to maximize your chances of receiving a really fair price.

So don't get carried away by the per share premiums. Instead focus on looking at things a month out and repeat the process every month. Furthermore, your own ability to predict what might happen a month from now is better than trying to predict what will happen a year or two out from today.

Lastly, remember to take taxes and commissions into account. I've highlighted the numbers before commissions but depending on your broker's fee structure, it might be more profitable to simply write options every two months instead of every month. A lot of option trading success is all about basic math, so don't hesitate to run the numbers.

A top tip for you is to hold your long position for a little while in order to get used to its movements before beginning to write calls on it. Don't be in a rush to start earning the interest. Remember, your long position is the primary generator of gains so you should seek to preserve this position for as long as possible.

The covered call will decrease your cost basis and will therefore really add to your gains in the long run. You'll be able to stomach more gyrations in the stock beyond your original price thanks to the income you're earning.

Chapter 8:
How to Use the Collar Strategy

Are you enjoying the book? I would be really happy if you could leave me a short review on Amazon to get your opinion!

While the covered call is useful for those who wish to look at their stock holdings with an investment perspective, the covered call is for those who wish to only speculate. On the surface of it, this strategy is more complex than the previous one but this is just a veneer. You'll find that it is a versatile strategy to deploy.

In addition to this, if you hold a long stock position with substantial unrealized gains, you can consider executing a collar.

Collars

The collar strategy is an extremely flexible way of trading that you can use for either short term or long-term positions. Mind you, when using it for long term positions, make sure you have substantial unrealized gains already present. This is because the collar imposes a maximum gain limit.

On the flip side, it also caps your downside loss, so this lends itself very well to short term speculative strategies. Mind you, when I say short term, I'm still talking about holding onto the position for at least a month to take advantage of the time decay. From a longer term investment perspective, if you have a position which has made you a lot of money but you're either unsure of how it's going to perform over the short term or are not sure if it will move much further over the long term, you can use the collar to squeeze out the last drops of income from the trade or let it take you out.

This strategy introduces an additional layer on complexity since it has three legs to it:

1. A long stock positions

2. A long protective or married put

3. A short-covered call

In essence, we're adding a long protective put to the covered call strategy. This helps cover the downside and adds to the advantages that a covered call has.

Execution

The first leg to establish is the long stock leg. Like with the covered call, this is an income generator and is entered with the thought of having it increase in value. The second leg to enter is the married put. A married put is a put that covers your downside. Think of it as a stop loss order. Your maximum loss is capped to this level.

The put is bought at an out of the money price (that is below current market levels) at a price that is equal to your maximum risk limit for that position. So if you think you want to risk a move of just 5 points, then the put is purchased at that price.

Lastly, you need to write an out of the money call just like with the covered call. This call is covered by your long stock position. Make sure you execute your position in this exact order so that you minimize your risk. Let's work through the scenarios on this trade.

If your stock decreases in value, the put below it caps your maximum loss. Once the stock goes below the put's strike price, thereby moving it into the money, that leg is going to be in a profit no matter how low the stock's price goes. If you wish to exit, you sell your stock and you can sell your put which would have increased in value.

Alternatively, if the stock increases in value but doesn't hit your call's strike price before expiry, you earn the premium and the capital gain but are out the amount you paid to buy the put. If the stock does hit the call's strike price, this is your maximum gain possible on the stock leg and you'll have to sell your stock at the call's strike price.

In this case you again earn the capital gains on the long stock leg and the premium on the covered call leg but are out the premium you paid for buying the put. In addition to this, there are alternative scenarios you can encounter.

Let's say the stock declines in value but you're not sure that this is a long-term thing. You feel it's a temporary blip and it'll soon turn upwards. So what do you do? Should you exit all three positions? Well, this is where the decision to adjust your trade comes into play. You can either reestablish the collar at different prices, which is change the strike prices of the call and the put, or you can exit altogether.

Technical and fundamental analysis should play a part in your decision. I'll look at this in detail in a later section in this chapter. For now, just keep in mind that the collar is a wonderfully flexible strategy and with adjustment you can make money even when the trade goes against you or if something unexpected happens.

Now, let's look at an example with real numbers to see how it all plays out.

Example

Sticking with GOOG, we see that the market price is still $1229. So as a first step, in case this is a speculative position, we establish the long stock leg. Next, we establish the long put or protective put. Which price should you choose? Remember, this is an option purchase, so you'll need to pay to enter the position. The temptation will be to enter at as low a price as possible since you're going to lose this money no matter what happens (if it moves into the money or remains out of the money you lose the option premium no matter what). Resist the temptation to look at this in monetary terms.

Instead look at it in terms of risk involved. Your put's strike price will dictate your maximum position size. You need to decide what your necessary risk per trade amount is going to be. This can be a function of either a percentage of your overall capital or a fixed amount.

Once this is done, you divide this amount by the points between your put and the long stock entry point and this gives you your position size. Simple math really. Place your put at a level beyond the closest support which you think is going to hold. The idea is to not have this put move into the money, not minimize the cost you pay.

Remember that this trade is only going to last a little beyond a month so don't go searching for the stronger support out there. Simply pick the most appropriate one given the current balance in the market. For example, if it's in a range, simply pick a level which is beyond the lower range boundary.

Let's say you decide to enter GOOG at the current market price and that an appropriate put level is 1200. Looking at GOOG's option chain, we see that the October 25th 1200 put is selling for $25.20. So this amount is going to go out of pocket, in addition to whatever you paid for the long stock.

Now, we search for an appropriate level to write our call. It is yielding the same price as before and that is $16. We will receive this amount no matter what.

Hence, our cost of entry equals:

Cost of entry = cost of long stock price + cost of put premium - premium received from short call = 1229+25.2-16 = 1238.20 per share

You'll notice how the cost on entry actually increases with this method as opposed to a straight long stock purchase. Well, this is the price you pay for the additional protection. If you were to merely protect your downside via a put, your breakeven price would increase by the value of the put premium. In this case, that works out to $25.20.

So the covered call reduces your breakeven price quite significantly while maintaining your downside as intended. All in all, you pay a few dollars more for this privilege which is a good deal overall. Now that we know our cost of entry, what is our maximum loss?

Maximum loss = Long stock entry - Put strike price - premium from call + put premium paid = 1229-1200-16+25.2 = $38.20 per share.

If you placed a stop loss order at the put's strike price wouldn't that cover your downside for a lesser amount? Yes, but remember that the put insulates you from the possibility of the market price jumping your stop loss level thanks to a lack of liquidity or excess volatility. So, there is a price to pay for this protection. Let's see how your maximum gain is affected.

Maximum gain = Call strike price - Long stock entry price - put entry premium + call writing premium = 1270-1229-25.2+16 = $31.80 per share

In these calculations, the premiums you pay and receive for the options skew the numbers quite a lot. In reality, a lot of options strategies do not take the premiums paid into account when figuring out the maximum gain and risk because this is a cash expense. However, I'm illustrating these here just to show you how it affects the numbers.

So it looks like you're risking a larger amount than what you stand to gain when you take the premiums into account. Two things about this: this is just an example and I've assumed certain price levels so this is not fully reflective of the strategy. Second, this highlights the importance of picking a good put and call strike price level since the premiums do skew the numbers quite a lot.

This is why it's extremely important for you to brush up on your technical analysis skills prior to trading collars. You can get away with imperfect knowledge when it comes to the covered call since that has a large long stock leg which makes you all the money. However, over here your holding time is shorter and your transaction costs are higher.

Hence, get to know the stock you're trading deeply and simulate collars on it before going live. The collar should really be the cornerstone of your options trading strategy so make sure you master this before moving onto the other strategies in this book. In terms of progression, I would say do not move ahead until you're making steady money with collars.

On the plus side, once you've established the collar, it needs no maintenance and pretty much takes care of itself. This doesn't mean you switch off from the market completely. I'd suggest checking in at least once a day, which is the minimum required for passive trading strategies.

The collar as you can see is a long-biased strategy. Is it possible to have a bearish collar? Well, yes, it is actually. Now that you've grasped the basics of the execution required as well as the math that underlies the strategy, let's look at what to do in case you wish to adjust the trade.

Adjustments

So you've entered a collar and promptly the price dives below your entry and brings your put into the money. What now? You were envisioning holding onto the position for at least a month but here you are, less than a day in the trade, and you're already facing the prospect of hitting your maximum loss.

The first thing to do is to evaluate whether your technical assumptions are still valid. If your technical analysis was spot on, usually there will be some fundamental event you have overlooked. Is your stock dependent on the bond market, unbeknownst to you? Check your assumptions once again and see if your entry logic still holds water. If it doesn't, eat the loss and move on. Chalk it up to the cost of tuition of learning how to trade.

By the way, expect to do this sort of thing quite a lot when you're starting out. Trading is not an easy endeavor and this is why you should make as many of your mistakes in simulation, while demoing your strategies, instead of jumping into a live account and sabotaging yourself.

Assuming your initial conclusions are still valid, perhaps this is a temporary downswing in an effort to shakeout the weaker long traders. In such cases, you can seek to reestablish your collar. First, sell your put position and determine what will be a more appropriate level to reenter. When you sell your put, you'll make money on that leg since it would have moved into the money. Hence you can profit from the temporary downswing in the market.

When determining a secondary put level, keep in mind your average risk. Remember, you're not selling your long position so your average risk amount per trade is still based on your initial put levels. The profit you earn from selling the put will add to your account balance so take this into account and determine a level which satisfies your new risk per trade amount.

For example, if you earn $450 from selling the put, add this to your initial account balance. So your new account balance is now x+450 where x is the original balance. Let's say your original put level was 5 points away and your position size is 10 shares.

What should the new put level be given the increased account balance and existing position size so that your risk per trade remains similar? Well, this is simple arithmetic. Divide your new risk per trade with your position size to arrive at the stop loss or put strike price distance.

Once the secondary put has been established, you need to check whether you wish to leave your covered call in place. If you choose to close this leg of the trade, you'll still clear a profit since the call's price would have decreased. Hence, you can simply cover your position by buying it back at a lower price.

If your initial assumptions are still valid, you shouldn't need to change your call level. However, you need to take into account the time factor. If there's just a week remaining for the call to expire, perhaps it's best to establish the collar in the next month thanks to the time decay.

Take special care that you establish the option legs in the same expiry month. When adjusting the position, it is very easy to establish the secondary put in the current month and the call in the near month. Hopefully, I don't need to explain why this makes no sense for you. The point is to have downside protection throughout the trade and if it expires midway through, you have a problem, not a collar.

As an added precaution, have rough secondary levels marked out beforehand when you enter the collar. Don't execute it blindly but evaluate to see if your assumptions still hold. With this risk plan in hand you'll be prepared to act decisively when something unexpected happens and the trade goes against you.

In conclusion, the collar is the bedrock of all options trading strategies. This is not because other strategies derive anything from it. It's because of the fact that it tests your skills when it comes to everything related to options trading. You need to have good technical analysis skills, you need to be able to estimate proper strike price using s/r, and you need to adjust your trade when the unexpected happens.

So as I said before, make sure you're making money with this strategy before moving ahead. Simulate it extensively and really get to know the stocks you're speculating in. Understand that the other strategies don't necessarily make more money. They're just more creative and different ones will appeal to different traders.

It is perfectly possible to make excellent money executing a bunch of collars in multiple stocks. So don't think you need to progress to something or that you cannot be successful doing just one thing.

Between covered calls and collars, we've covered the entry level strategies for those looking to trade options. One downside of both of these strategies is that they need capital. The most expensive portion of these trades is the long stock position and this is what makes you money, so it's not as if you can skip it entirely.

All the remaining strategies in this book do not need any long stock position to succeed. This is why I labeled them 'creative'. We'll start by looking at the Iron Condor. Despite the alarming name, trust me, this is a wonderful strategy to employ in the markets.

Underneath it, it's actually covered. Hence, why we call them covered calls and such because the stock is underneath there.

The concept is for only advanced traders because it does involve a lot of profit potential. Yes, but also a risk, and you need to have money management as well. You should understand the riskiness of this, and don't do it until you've got some experience underneath your belt.

So naked put means where you put a put option underneath there, without any stock. The risk exposure is essentially the main difference between this and a naked call.

Naked puts are used when the investor expects the stock to be above the strike price at the time of the expiration. Similar to naked calls, the potential for print is limited to the premium that you have. A person can make the most of the stock if it's traded above the strike price at the expiration, and it expires and becomes worthless. If this happens, you're keeping the entire premium.

While this has unlimited risk in some ways, that's actually not the case. The risk of the naked put is different from the call, in that the trader could lose most if the stock goes all the way to zero. There is still significant risk there when compared to the reward you get, and unlike the naked call, if this does get exercised against you, you'll get the receiving stock. This is opposed to getting a short position on the stock, as in the case of the naked call, and you can hold the stock as part of the possible exit strategies as well.

So what is the risk? Well, there is the risk that you could end up having to pay for all of the stock, and if it plummets, you're going to end up being stuck with a dying ship, that's for sure.

As an example, let's take stock X, and let's say that you see it trade on March 1st at about $45 a share. So, for the sake of simplicity, and let's assume that they may $44 puts are over there at $1. If we sell that, we'll get a $100 for every single put that's sold. If it trades above the $44 share at expiration, it will then be worthless, and we'll get $100 for every single option sold.

But, let's say that it falls below the price of that when it expires. Well, we can from there except for the Y to be assigned to our stock, with 100 shares of that, at the price of $44, so it will cost about $4400 for everything. If you're looking to potentially have the cost basis at say $43, a share, you'll immediately see the losses there.

However, contrary to naked call, you'll see the max loss on this being $4300 on this, and it would only be if the stock went to zero, which is unlikely in the index, but possible if you have individual stock.

Usually, these requirements for this are a little more accommodating, and that's because if the put is exercised and you get the stock, as opposed to short stacking, as in the naked call, the maximum risk exposure is the value of the stock position and is less than what the premium received for the put option is.

This is a risky process, and it may seem like easy money, but that's far from the case. It's an exact science, so remember that next time you consider doing this type of trade.

Puts are a good way to get some different investments, just make sure that you know what you're doing, and you understand the market before you try most of this.

Chapter 9: Market Environment

At this point, you have nine strategies to trade options for all kinds of market conditions, be it neutral, bearish, or bullish. While the strategies by themselves will limit your risk and give you rewards according to their risk profiles, the biggest risk in all of these is you applying the wrong strategy to the wrong market conditions.

There's no strategy that can completely eliminate the risk of you making a mistake, unfortunately. Even a neutral strategy, like the straddle or strangle, will not work if you misread a range for a trend.

Technical and fundamental analysis will help you determine what market conditions are appropriate. While every trader has different perspectives on this, personally, I tend to lean more towards technical analysis when it comes to determining which stocks to operate in. This is because fundamental analysis favors longer timelines, of over 5 years, for investment purposes. While the earnings announcements are important, a fundamentally low valuation doesn't play itself out over the course of a few months.

Thus, I'll be focusing mostly on technical analysis methods from here on out. Before we get to all of that though, you need to understand some basics about the market environment: namely, what is a trend and what is a range.

Trends and Ranges

The market is a chaotic place with a number of traders vying for dominance over one another. There are a countless number of strategies and time frames in play and at any point, it is close to impossible to determine who will emerge with the upper hand. In such an environment, how is it then possible to make any money? After all, if everything is unpredictable, how can you get your picks right?

Well, this is where thinking in terms of probabilities comes into play. While you cannot get every single bet right, as long as you get enough right and make enough money on those to offset your losses, you will make money in the long run. This goes back to what I spoke about in the risk management chapter.

It's not about getting one or two right. It's about executing the strategy with the best odds of winning over and over again, and ensuring that your math works out with regards to the relationship between your win rate and average win.

So it really comes down to finding patterns which repeat themselves over time in the markets. What causes these patterns? Well, the other traders of course! To put it more accurately, the orders that the other traders place in the market are what creates patterns that repeat themselves over time.

The first step to understanding these patterns is to understand what trends and ranges are. Identifying them and learning to spot when they transition into one another will give you a massive leg up not only with your options trading but also with directional trading.

Trends

In theory spotting a trend is simple enough. Look left to right and if the price is headed up or down, it's a trend. Well, sometimes it is really that simple. However, for the majority of the time you have both with and counter-trend forces operating in the market. It is possible to have long counter trend reactions within a larger trend and sometimes, depending on the time frame you're in, these counter-trend reactions take up the majority of your screen space.

Trend vs Range

This is a chart of the UK100 CFD, which mimics the FTSE 100, on the four-hour time frame. Three-quarters of the chart is a downtrend and the last quarter is a wild uptrend. Using the looking left to right guideline, we'd conclude that this instrument is in a range. Is that really true though?

Just looking at that chart, you can clearly see that short-term momentum is bullish. So if you were considering taking a trade on this, would you implement a range strategy or a trending one? This is exactly the sort of thing that catches traders up.

The key to deciphering trends is to watch for two things: counter trend participation quality and turning points. Let's tackle counter trend participation first.

Counter Trend Participation

When a new trend begins, the market experiences extremely imbalanced order flow which is tilted towards one side. There's isn't much counter trend participation against this seeming tidal wave of with trend orders. Price marches on without any opposition and experiences only a few hiccups.

As time goes on though, the with trend forces run out of steam and have to take breaks to gather themselves. This is where counter trend traders start testing the trend and trying to see how far back into the trend they can go. While it is unrealistic to expect a full reversal at this point, the quality of the correction or pushback tells us a lot about the strength distribution between the with and counter-trend forces.

Eventually, the counter-trend players manage to push so far back against the trend that a stalemate results in the market. The with and counter-trend forces are equally balanced and thus the trend comes to an end. After all, you need an imbalance for the market to tip one way or another and a balanced order flow is only going to result in a sideways market.

While all this is going on behind the scenes, the price chart is what records the push and pull between these two forces. Using the price chart, we can not only anticipate when a trend is coming to an end but also how long it could potentially take before it does. This second factor, which helps us estimate the time it could take, is invaluable from an options perspective, especially if you're using a horizontal spread strategy.

Here's what you look out for to gauge counter trend participation:

1. QUALITY OF COUNTER-TREND CANDLES- ARE THEY STRONG/WEAK/HAVE WICKS/SMALL BODIED, ETC.?

2. NUMBER OF COUNTER-TREND CANDLES WITHIN THE MOVEMENT- IS THIS CHANGING OVER TIME?

3. LENGTH OF PUSHBACKS- ARE THE PUSHBACKS INCREASING IN NUMBER? ARE THEY LASTING FOR LONGER?

In all cases, the greater the number of them, the greater the counter-trend participation in the market. The closer a trend is to ending, the greater the counter-trend participation. Thus, the minute you begin to see price move into a large, sideways move with an equal number of buyers and sellers in it, you can be sure that some form of redistribution is going on.

Mind you, the trend might continue or reverse. Either way, it doesn't matter. What matters is that you know the trend is weak and that now is probably not the time to be banking on trend strategies.

Starting from the left, we can see that there is close to no counter trend bars, bearish in this case, and the bulls make easy progress. Note the angle with which the bulls proceed upwards. Then comes the first major correction and the counter-trend players push back against the last third of the bull move. Notice how strong the bearish bars are and note their character compared to the bullish bars.

The bulls recover and push the price higher at the original angle and without any bearish presence, which seems odd. This is soon explained as the bears slam price back down and for a while, it looks as if they've managed to form a V top reversal in the trend, which is an extremely rare occurrence.

The price action that follows is a more accurate reflection of the power in the market, with both bulls and bears sharing chunks of the order flow, with overall order flow in the bull's favor but only just. Price here is certainly in an uptrend but looking at the extent of the bearish pushbacks, perhaps we should be on our guard for a bearish reversal. After all order flow is looking pretty sideways at this point.

So how would we approach an options strategy with the chart in the state it is in at the extreme right? Well, for one, any strategy that requires an option beyond the near month is out of the question, given the probability of it turning. Secondly, looking at the order flow, it does seem to be following a channel, doesn't it?

While the channel isn't very clean, if you were aggressive enough, you could consider deploying a collar with the strike prices above and below this channel to take advantage of the price movement. You could also employ some moderately bullish strategies as price approaches the bottom of this channel and figuring out the extent of the bull move is easier thanks to you being able to reference the top of the channel.

As price moves in this channel, it's all well and good. Eventually though, we know that the trend has to flip. How do we know when this happens?

Turning Points

As bulls and bears struggle over who gets to control the order flow, price swings up and down. You will notice that every time price comes back into the 6427-6349 zone, the bulls seem to step in masse and repulse the bears.

This tells us that the bulls are willing to defend this level in large numbers and strongly at that. Given the number of times the bears have tested this level, we can safely assume that above this level, bullish strength is a bit weak. However, at this level, it is as if the bulls have retreated and are treating this as a sort of last resort, for the trend to be maintained. You can see where I'm going with this.

If this level were to be breached by the bears, it is a good bet that a large number of bulls will be taken out. In martial terms, the largest army of bulls has been marshaled at this level. If this force is defeated, it is unlikely that there's going to be too much resistance to the bears below this level.

This zone, in short, is a turning point. If price breaches this zone decisively, we can safely assume that the bears have moved in and control the majority if the order flow.

Turning Point Breached

The decisive turning point zone is marked by the two horizontal lines and the price touches this level twice more and is repulsed by the bulls. Notice how the last bounce before the level breaks produces an extremely weak bullish bounce and price simply caves through this. Notice the strength with which the bears break through.

The FTSE was in a longer uptrend on the weekly chart so the bulls aren't completely done yet. However, as far as the daily timeframe is concerned, notice how price retests that same level but this time around, it acts as resistance instead of support.

For now, we can conclude that as long as the price remains below the turning point, we are bearishly biased. You can see this by looking at the angle with which bulls push back as well as, the lack of strong bearish participation on the push upwards.

This doesn't mean we go ahead and pencil in a bull move and start implementing strategies that take advantage of the upcoming bullish move. Remember, nothing is for certain in the markets. Don't change your bias or strategy until the turning point decisively breaks.

Some key things to note here are that a turning point is always a major S/R level. It is usually a swing point where a large number of with trend forces gather to support the trend. This will not always be the case, so don't make the mistake of hanging on to older turning points.

The current order flow and price action are what matters the most, so pay attention to that above all else. Also, note how the candles that test this level all have wicks on top of them.

This indicates that the bears are quite strong here and that any subsequent attack will be handled the same way until the level breaks. Do we know when the level will break? Well, we can't say with any accuracy. However, we can estimate the probability of it breaking.

The latest upswing has seen very little bearish pushback, comparatively speaking, and the push into the level is strong. Instinct would say that there's one more rejection left here. However, who knows? Until the level breaks, we stay bearish. When the level breaks, we switch to the bullish side.

Putting it all Together

So now we're ready to put all of this together into one coherent package. Your analysis should always begin with determining the current state of the market. Ranges are pretty straightforward to spot and they occur either within big pullbacks in trends or at the end of trends.

Trends vary in strength depending on the amount of counter-trend participation they have. The way to determine counter trend participation levels is to simply look at the price bars and compare the counter-trend ones to the with trend ones. The angle with which the trend progresses is a great gauge as well, for its strength, with steeper angles being stronger.

Next, you need to determine the turning point of the trend. The turning point is a level that is extremely well defended by the with trend players and will be attacked repeatedly by the counter-trend traders in long trends.

Once you have the turning point figured out, you need to then stick to your bias and let the S/R guide you with regards to strike prices for your options strategies. Reading support and resistance is an essential skill you must master. So let's look at this in more detail.

Chapter 10:
Rules for Successful Trading

Ensuring dependable profits in the financial markets is much more difficult than it seems at first glance. It is assessed that over 75% of all members in the end wash out and take up more secure side interests. Be that as it may, the financier business once in a while distributes customer disappointment rates, since they're concerned reality may drive away new records, so the washout rate could be a lot higher.

The Road to Long-Term Profitability

Long haul benefit requires two interrelated ranges of abilities. To begin with, we need techniques that get more cash-flow than they lose. Second, those techniques must perform well while the market shape-moves through bull and bear driving forces, with a lot of uneven periods in the middle. While numerous brokers realize how to profit in explicit economic situations, similar to a solid upturn, they bomb over the long haul on the grounds that their techniques don't adjust to unavoidable changes.

So would you be able to split away from the pack and unite the expert minority with a methodology that raises your chances for long haul success? Begin with an unmistakable and succinct arrangement.

1. Disregard the Holy Grail

Losing brokers fantasize about the mystery recipe that will mysteriously improve their outcomes. As a general rule, there are no mysteries in light of the fact that the way to progress consistently goes through cautious decision, viable risk the executives, and gifted benefit taking.

2. Connect with Your Trading Plan

Update your trading plan week by week or month to month to incorporate new thoughts and kill awful ones. Return and read the arrangement at whatever point you fall in an opening and are searching for an approach to get out.

3. Be careful with Reinforcement

Dynamic trading discharges adrenaline and endorphins. These synthetics can create sentiments of happiness notwithstanding when you are losing cash. Thus, this urges addictive characters to take terrible positions, just to get the hurry.

4. Try not to Cut Corners

Your opposition burns through many hours consummating methodologies and you are in for a severe shock in the event that you hope to toss a couple of darts and leave with a benefit. It's far more terrible in the event that you cut corners in a mind-blowing remainder since that unfortunate propensity is a lot harder to break.

5. Grasp Simplicity

Concentrate on value activity, understanding that everything else is optional. Feel free to assemble complex specialized markers yet remember their essential capacity is to affirm or disprove what you're prepared eye as of now observes.

6. Evade the Obvious

Benefit infrequently pursues the greater part. When you see an ideal exchange arrangement, almost certainly, every other person sees it too, planting you in the group and setting you up for disappointment.

7. Arrange Your Personal Life

Whatever is not right in your life will in the end persist into your trading execution. This is particularly risky on the off chance that you haven't profited, riches and the attractive extremity of plenitude and shortage.

8. Try not to Break Your Rules

You make trading principles to get you out of inconvenience when positions go seriously. On the off chance that you don't enable them to carry out their responsibility, you have lost your order and opened the entryway to significantly more noteworthy misfortunes.

9. Tune in to Your Intuition

Trading utilizes the scientific and imaginative sides of your cerebrum so you have to develop both to prevail over the long haul. When you are alright with math, you can upgrade results with reflection, a couple of yoga stances or a tranquil stroll in the recreation center.

10. Make Peace with Losses

Trading is one of only a handful couple of callings where losing cash each day is a characteristic way to progress. Each trading misfortune accompanies a significant market exercise in case you are available to the message.

11. Try not to Believe in a Company

In case you are excessively enamored with your trading vehicle, you offer approach to defective basic leadership. You must gain by wastefulness, profiting while every other person is inclining the incorrect way.

12. Lose the Crowd

Long haul productivity requires situating in front of or behind the group, yet never in the group since that is the place savage techniques target. Avoid stock sheets and visit rooms. This is not kidding business and everybody in those spots has an ulterior thought process.

13. Try not to try to Get Even

Drawdowns are a characteristic piece of the merchant's life cycle. Acknowledge them effortlessly and adhere to the reliable methodologies you realize will in the long run recover your presentation on track.

14. Try not to Count Your Chickens

Like an exchange that is going your direction yet the cash is not yours until you close out. Lock in what you can as ahead of schedule as possible, with trailing stops or fractional benefits, so concealed hands cannot pickpocket your prosperity ultimately.

15. Watch for Early Warnings

Huge misfortunes once in a while happen without various specialized admonitions. Dealers routinely overlook those signs and enable would like to supplant keen control, setting themselves up for torment.

16. Pursue Your Discipline

Order cannot be instructed in a workshop or found in costly trading programming. Dealers burn through a great many dollars attempting to make up for their absence of poise yet few understand that a long look in the mirror achieves a similar assignment at a lot less expensive cost!

17. Apparatuses Don't Think

Dealers compensate for deficient aptitudes with costly programming, prepackaged with a wide range of exclusive purchase and sell signals. These apparatuses meddle with important experience since you think the product is more brilliant than you are.

18. Play with Your Head

It's normal for dealers to copy their monetary saints but at the same time it's an ideal method to lose cash. Take in what you can from others, at that point back off and set up your very own market personality, in light of your one of a kind abilities and risk resistance.

19. Jettison the Paycheck Mentality

We're educated to pound through the stir week and afterward get our checks. This compensation for-exertion remunerate mindset clashes with the common progression of trading wins and misfortunes over the span of a year. Truth be told, insights show that most yearly benefits are set up for only a bunch of days the market is open for business.

20. Stay away from Market Gurus

It's your cash in question, not theirs. Remember that they're likely talking up their positions, trusting the energized prattle will expand their benefits, not yours.

Most by far of dealers neglect to tap their maximum capacity, in the end trading in for cold hard currency their chips and discovering progressively customary approaches to profit. Become a pleased individual from the expert minority by following exemplary principles intended to keep a well-honed spotlight on productivity.

Chapter 11:
Tips for Trading Options

Although most trading platforms are straightforward, it is important to always observe a few tips to ensure success. These vary from stock options to risk management and rules around taxation. Here are some of the best tips to keep you in the trade.

1. Learning

One great tip that can help you succeed in trading options is about education and research. If you interact with any expert in options trading, you will get to understand how important it is to collect and digest information. Just like any other trade, the options market keeps changing every day and you must stay apprised of these changes.

Several resources on this trade are available online for free download. One such useful resource is the Jeff Augend day trading options book. You should constantly acquire books, courses, PDFs and video tutorials to broaden your knowledge on options trading. You can also join chat rooms, blogs, and forums where trading options is the main topic for discussion.

2. Practice Accounts

It is often difficult to wait until you have mastered the trade before investing in it. However, getting to trade too early can cost you a lot in terms of capital. It is wise to start with a demo account as this will help you to improve on your trading plan and try out the platform before investing in it. Demo accounts are always funded using simulated cash so you do not need to worry about losing your capital.

3. Rules and regulations

Get to understand the rules and restrictions governing the markets within your country. For instance, the United States has FINRA rules that govern day trading of options. One of the regulations states that your account must have at least $25,000 for you to meet trade over four times in five business days. This only applies to the US.

4. Payment of tax

In some countries, you may be taxed for the profits you make trading options. Before you start trading, find out what your tax obligations will be to remain on the safe side of the business.

5. Risk management

It is essential to have a risk management strategy in place. This will help reduce losses and ensure that you remain in good standing, the trading options notwithstanding. Most experts advise that you apply the 1% rule in your transactions. The rule states that for every single trade you should not risk more than 1% of your capital. This means that if you have, for example, $20,000 in your account, the most you should trade is $200. Once you achieve consistent gain then you can start increasing the risk, gradually.

6. Automated software

If you have a good strategy in place, you may consider investing in automated software. This utilizes algorithms to trade on your behalf. One advantage of automation is that it helps you trade faster thus making more trades than if you did this manually. Nonetheless, for it to be successful you must have an effective strategy in place.

Take Away Points

Intraday trading has two major objectives. As usual, the first one is to make a profit. The second one is to do this with less or no risk. Options provide an ideal tool for achieving these two objectives without a struggle.

The overall design of options trading platforms makes it possible for you to set risk limits and make multiple transactions while maximizing profits. These advantages are missing in other financial instruments and you will be able to make awesome picks that place you at a competitive edge. In closing, echoing Robert Arnott who once said 'In investing, what is comfortable is rarely profitable', it is good to take a risk. You may lose at times, but not always.

Options trading is also used by many astute investors to either improve their portfolio, reduce the risk of owning a particular option or grow wealthy with less risk on their side as they leverage their knowledge in options to grow their portfolio and become a much more financial success. Over the century, the resilience of options trading in prevailing through all kinds of bad conations has proved too many people that it is one of the ways to trade in securities with the lowest risk possible with promising high returns.

19 - Conclusion

Now that you have been introduced to some of the basics of day trading, you can begin to understand the avenues that are available to you when it comes to trading on the stock market.

The steps outlined in this book are just the beginning, and to become a successful day trader you will need to do more than just study the markets and start picking up little nuances like different trends and how they affect stock prices.

There are many websites online that offer you the chance to try your hand at day trading on a simulator BEFORE you even start trading on a real market, and such websites are going to have to become an integral part of your study as you explore this field of trade.

Normal investors call day traders gamblers for a reason, and that is because every day really is a gamble. Good day traders have been known to make over US$ 150,000 a year, but that does not mean they did not have their bad days where they lost a few thousand in the wrong security.

Remember, good discipline, and good money management are key to being a good day trader. Also, not allowing your emotions to run away with you when it is time to make a trade, or when you have heard some news is also imperative. Try as hard as possible to be logical and thorough when it comes to your trading practices, and with time even you could be making a 6-figure salary from the comfort of your home.

Conclusion

Besides understanding the basics of options, the most important thing to learn is the wide range of strategies that can be used when it comes to options. These strategies open a lot of doors for traders to make profits that would not be available otherwise.

When you are learning, you should try out all the strategies to see what works best for you. Everyone is going to have their own tastes, but options trading is so different that you need to try things out before you get stuck only buying call options, which is a mistake that happens to a lot of beginners who are afraid to try the many different strategies that options trading has to offer.

One of my favorite things about options is that you can get involved in options trading without having very much money. If people were smart and disciplined about it, options trading could even provide a way out of a low-income situation. You can start trading with a hundred dollars, and if you are careful with it a year from now, there is no reason that you could not significantly grow that into a large trading account.

Just remember that options trading is a serious business, but it can be fun and exciting too. There is no reason why making money has to be tedious and difficult. You can get involved at the highest levels of our economy with the best companies, by trading options. Hopefully, you will be able to ride the wave on the stock market and earn some of your own profits.

Remember that options trading is flexible, so when the market enters a downturn, don't stop trading! You can keep going and earn profits as the share price goes down and everyone else is panicking.

Thank you again for taking the time to read this book, and if you have enjoyed the book, please leave a review for us on Amazon. We will enjoy hearing from you about your trading experiences!

© Copyright 2020 - All rights reserved.

The content contained within this book may not be reproduced, duplicated or transmitted without direct written permission from the author or the publisher.

Under no circumstances will any blame or legal responsibility be held against the publisher, or author, for any damages, reparation, or monetary loss due to the information contained within this book. Either directly or indirectly.

Legal Notice:
This book is copyright protected. This book is only for personal use. You cannot amend, distribute, sell, use, quote or paraphrase any part, or the content within this book, without the consent of the author or publisher.

Disclaimer Notice:
Please note the information contained within this document is for educational and entertainment purposes only. All effort has been executed to present accurate, up to date, and reliable, complete information. No warranties of any kind are declared or implied. Readers acknowledge that the author is not engaging in the rendering of legal, financial, medical or professional advice. The content within this book has been derived from various sources. Please consult a licensed professional before attempting any techniques outlined in this book.

By reading this document, the reader agrees that under no circumstances is the author responsible for any losses, direct or indirect, which are incurred as a result of the use of information contained within this document, including, but not limited to, — errors, omissions, or inaccuracies.

www.ingramcontent.com/pod-product-compliance
Lightning Source LLC
Chambersburg PA
CBHW071411210526
45465CB00001B/342